Mobile Devices and Technology in Higher Education

This book examines key issues at the intersection of education and technology by addressing the question that most educators face—how do we use technology to engage students in the learning process and enhance learning?

Problematizing the view that technology is the default solution to a host of problems facing education, while also recognizing that technology has an important place in a variety of education levels, the book provides readers with clear insights on technology and learning from a variety of perspectives from communication studies, education, and related disciplines.

This volume is an essential read for scholars and teachers working in the area of elementary education. It will also be of interest to academics working in the area of education, postsecondary education, and learning and can be used as an ancillary text in graduate-level seminars.

Jeffrey H. Kuznekoff is an Associate Professor in the Department of Interdisciplinary and Communication Studies at Miami University. His research examines new communication technology, instructional communication, and communication occurring within multiplayer gaming. His research has been published in *Communication Education*, *New Media and Society*, and *PLOS one*.

Stevie M. Munz is an Assistant Professor in the Department of Communication at Utah Valley University. Her research explores how human beings understand and communicate the experiences of identity, power, politics, and gender in classrooms and small-town communities. Her work appears in *Departures*, *Communication Education*, *Women & Language*, and the *Western Journal of Communication*.

Scott Titsworth is the Dean of the Scripps College of Communication at Ohio University. He has developed an international reputation as a leading scholar in the area of classroom communication effectiveness. He has more than 50 books, chapters, and articles published on the topic.

NCA Focus on Communication Studies
National Communication Association

The Twitter Presidency
Donald J. Trump and the Politics of White Rage
Brian L. Ott & Greg Dickinson

Mobile Devices and Technology in Higher Education
Jeffrey H. Kuznekoff, Stevie M. Munz, and Scott Titsworth

Mobile Devices and Technology in Higher Education

Jeffrey H. Kuznekoff, Stevie M. Munz, and Scott Titsworth

NEW YORK AND LONDON

First published 2020
by Routledge
52 Vanderbilt Avenue, New York, NY 10017

and by Routledge
2 Park Square, Milton Park, Abingdon, Oxon, OX14 4RN

Routledge is an imprint of the Taylor & Francis Group, an informa business

© 2020 Taylor & Francis

The right of Jeffrey H. Kuznekoff, Stevie M. Munz, and Scott Titsworth to be identified as authors of this work has been asserted by them in accordance with sections 77 and 78 of the Copyright, Designs and Patents Act 1988.

All rights reserved. No part of this book may be reprinted or reproduced or utilised in any form or by any electronic, mechanical, or other means, now known or hereafter invented, including photocopying and recording, or in any information storage or retrieval system, without permission in writing from the publishers.

Trademark notice: Product or corporate names may be trademarks or registered trademarks, and are used only for identification and explanation without intent to infringe.

Library of Congress Cataloging-in-Publication Data
Names: Kuznekoff, Jeffrey H., author. | Munz, Stevie M., author. | Titsworth, Scott, author.
Title: Mobile devices and technology in higher education /
Jeffrey H. Kuznekoff, Stevie M. Munz, and Scott Titsworth.
Description: New York, NY: Routledge, 2020 |
Includes bibliographical references and index.
Identifiers: LCCN 2019026337 (print) | LCCN 2019026338 (ebook) |
ISBN 9780367375614 (hardback) | ISBN 9780429355097 (ebook)
Subjects: LCSH: Education, Higher—Effect of technological innovations on. |
Mobile communication systems in education. |
Education, Higher—Computer-assisted instruction. |
Educational technology. | Internet in education.
Classification: LCC LB2395.7 .K94 2020 (print) | LCC LB2395.7 (ebook) |
DDC 378.1/7344678—dc23
LC record available at https://lccn.loc.gov/2019026337
LC ebook record available at https://lccn.loc.gov/2019026338

ISBN: 978-0-367-37561-4 (hbk)
ISBN: 978-0-429-35509-7 (ebk)

Typeset in Sabon
by codeMantra

Contents

PART 1
Overview 1

  1 Overview 3

PART 2
Challenges to Student Learning 7

  2 Reducing Student Attention, Recall, and Note-taking 9
  3 Problematizing the "Digital Native" 18
  4 Digital Inequality and Digital Literacy Skills 24

PART 3
Technology in the Classroom 35

  5 The Active Classroom 37
  6 From Hardcopy to e-Book and e-Textbook Platforms 49
  7 Online Learning 58

PART 4
Technology and Academic Audiences 67

  8 Considerations for Teachers 69
  9 Considerations for Administrators 77

vi *Contents*

10 Considerations for Students   83

11 Conclusion   87

Index   91

Part 1
Overview

1 Overview

The Potential of the Modern Classroom

This chapter begins our discussion of the intersection between technology and education, in higher education. We argue that mobile devices and technology certainly can be used as tools to effectively enhance student learning; however, this is often a fairly complex process. In order to understand this process in more depth, we will need to explore the variety of issues that connect technology and learning.

Technology in the classroom is both enabling and constraining. On the one hand, technology can allow instructors to engage students in course content beyond the confines of the traditional classroom or in ways that can enhance learning. This occurs at all levels of education, from kindergarten to doctoral-level coursework. Children can learn their ABCs through interactive applications that provide visual and auditory feedback. Medical students can use virtual reality (VR) headsets, such as the Oculus Rift, to visually explore the body and understand human anatomy in an interactive way. College students can potentially carry around their entire personal textbook library on their iPad and take searchable, electronic notes. In elementary school, students can create HD movies that not only allow them to engage with course content, and demonstrate their understanding of course material, but also help them to develop the experience and skills needed for the twenty-first century. In addition, collaborative capabilities allow students to work in groups to share their understanding and knowledge with others. The list of ways that technology can, and has, fundamentally impacted learning is nearly endless.

Despite the promise of technology as a revolutionary education tool, we would argue that technology only helps to enable learning when it has carefully been considered and integrated into the curriculum

4 Overview

in a meaningful way. Often times, instructors or administrators may see the latest app or device and immediately want to use that in the classroom. However, such an approach may not be best for students, particularly if that technology comes across as a gimmick, without actual educational benefit.

This drive to integrate technology into education also has a significant connection to the economy. By 2013, spending on elementary through high school classrooms hardware reached $13 billion worldwide and is expected to increase to nearly $20 billion by 2020 (Nagel, 2014). Other estimates report that international investments toward education technology reached $9.5 billion in 2017 (Shulman, 2018), and still others forecast that the global educational technology market will reach over $40 billion by 2022 (Bhattacharyya, 2019). At the college level, we have seen programs developed to add technology to the college classroom. Ohio State University (OSU) is working with Apple to give new first-year students iPad Pros and accessories (Apple Pencil and Smart Keyboard), in addition to apps, to be used in their college-level courses and throughout their time at OSU (Davey, 2017). By 2019, that initiative had adapted to revisions made by Apple and selected a newly released iPad Air as the device they would be distributing to incoming students (Buchholz, 2019). The L.A Unified School District bought tens of thousands of iPads for use in the classroom (Blume, 2015). The school district later abandoned this effort and sought a refund from vendors.

The Problem with Technology and Learning

At the same time though, this multibillion dollar push toward integrating technology into every aspect of the classroom has created important questions and criticisms from a variety of audiences. Instead of technology being a panacea for education and sparking a massive growth in learning, we are finding that the connection is not simple. We run into skill gaps and the assumption that because millennials are "digital natives," they simply know how to use technology. We also assume that students all have mobile devices that are capable of doing what we need them to do. From our experience, it appears that this relationship between technology and learning is a complex one and certainly not as simple as it may appear. The initial thought that increasing the use of technology in learning will lead to an explosion of growth appears to be too optimistic. Instead, research has found that technology and learning have a complex relationship that needs to be understood in order for true learning to occur. Research, from a

Overview 5

variety of disciplines, has examined the relationship between technology and learning, particularly how technology may help to enhance learning outcomes. For example, research has found that 42% of students' time spent on laptops in class was spent on non-course related activities (Kraushaar & Novak, 2010) and that students tended to underreport the amount of distracting behaviors they engaged in. Two other studies examining mobile devices in the classroom have found that actively texting during a class lecture, about content unrelated to the class content, negatively affected student learning, note-taking, and recall of information (Kuznekoff & Titsworth, 2013). However, if students responded to or created messages that were related to class content, they did not suffer as much of a decrease in student learning as unrelated messages (Kuznekoff, Munz, & Titsworth, 2015). Additional research, discussed in the chapters that follow, will help to explore this complex relationship and shed additional light on how technology affects learning.

Summary

Technology has the ability to both enable and constrain learning. In order to effectively integrate any technology to enhance student learning, we need to understand this enabling and constraining dynamic and make careful decisions regarding how to proceed. That is the goal of this book, to examine this dynamic carefully and from a variety of viewpoints to help enable decision making at a variety of levels and inform this continuing conversation about technology, learning, and what the twenty-first century classroom will develop into. The first few chapters of this book (Part 2) discuss how technology in the classroom may be a challenge or determent to student learning. In particular, Chapter 2 examines how technology may negatively affect student learning. Chapter 3 shifts to a discussion of the term "digital native" and challenges the assumptions we have about college students and their competence with technology. Lastly, Chapter 4 goes in depth on the important issues of digital inequality and digital literacy skills. Next, Part 3 of this book examines technology in the classroom in a variety of different ways. Chapter 5 examines the active classroom and provides detailed examples of how technology can be a powerful educational tool and experience for students. Chapter 6 problematizes the recent shift from traditional paper textbooks to newer e-Book and e-Textbook platforms. Chapter 7 then shifts to various perspectives regarding online learning. Completing this book is Part 4, which focuses exclusively on considerations for a variety of

6 Overview

audiences. Chapters 8 through 10 focus on a different target audience within higher education, providing each with considerations as they contemplate technology and education.

References

Bhattacharyya, M. (2019, April 2). GOOGL, AAPL, MSFT & AMZN look to keep up with the edtech fad. Retrieved from https://www.nasdaq.com/article/googl-aapl-msft-amp-amzn-look-to-keep-up-with-the-edtech-fad-cm1123412

Blume, H. (2015, April 16). *L.A. school district demands iPad refund from Apple.* Retrieved from https://www.latimes.com/local/lanow/la-me-ln-ipad-curriculum-refund-20150415-story.html

Buchholz, G. (2019, March 28). iPad Air selected for 2019 distribution. Retrieved from https://digitalflagship.osu.edu/news/2019/03/28/ipad-air-selected-2019-distribution

Davey, C. (2017, October 4). Ohio State collaborates with Apple to launch digital learning initiative: Students, faculty, staff and community to gain access to new educational and economic development opportunities. Retrieved from https://news.osu.edu/news/2017/10/04/digital-flagship/

Kraushaar, J. M., & Novak, D. C. (2010). Examining the affects of student multitasking with laptops during the lecture. *Journal of Information Systems Education, 21,* 241–251.

Kuznekoff, J. H., Munz, S. M., & Titsworth, B. S. (2015). Mobile phones in the classroom: Examining the effects of texting, Twitter, and message content on student learning. *Communication Education, 64,* 344–365. doi:10.1080/03634523.2015.1038727

Kuznekoff, J. H., & Titsworth, B. S. (2013). The impact of mobile phone usage on student learning. *Communication Education, 62,* 233–252. doi: 10.1080/03634523.2013.767917

Nagel, D. (2014, June 11). Spending on instructional tech to reach $19 billion within 5 years. Retrieved from https://thejournal.com/articles/2014/06/11/spending-on-instructional-tech-to-reach-19-billion-within-5-years.aspx

Shulman, R. D. (2018, January 26). EdTech investments rise to a historical $9.5 billion: What your startup needs to know. Retrieved from https://www.forbes.com/sites/robynshulman/2018/01/26/edtech-investments-rise-to-a-historical-9-5-billion-what-your-startup-needs-to-know/#38f62a093a38

Part 2

Challenges to Student Learning

2 Reducing Student Attention, Recall, and Note-taking

Introduction

A wide variety of studies, across multiple disciplines, has examined the intersection of technology in the classroom. One particularly fruitful area of research has been the negative effects of technology on learning. This chapter summarizes several research agendas that have looked at mobile phones and computers in the classroom, particularly the negative influence of these devices on students learning.

In the United States, and indeed in many countries, the rapid development of new technology has greatly influenced our educational institutions and without question, many of these influences have been positive ones. For example, online course registration has replaced the days of waiting in line to physically register for a college class, and access to electronic library resources and scholarly journals provides faculty and students with tremendous access to a wide variety of sources on nearly any subject.

Despite the potential for technology to enhance learning and engage students in course material, a variety of studies across multiple disciplines demonstrate that technology can negatively influence learning. Our own research (Kuznekoff, Munz, & Titsworth, 2015; Kuznekoff & Titsworth, 2013) has examined how mobile phones negatively impact student attention, recall, and note-taking behaviors; however, the potential negative effects of technology in learning go well beyond research in the communication discipline.

Of primary interest to this chapter is examining ways in which technology in higher education may negatively affect student learning. This certainly does not mean that there is no hope for technology, indeed we each use technology in our classes on a fairly regular basis. However, technology cannot and must not be seen as a panacea for education in general, such a point of view is often met with failure.

10 Challenges to Student Learning

For example, in 2013, the L.A. Unified School District developed an iPad program that saw the purchase of over 40,000 iPads to be used in a curriculum developed by Pearson and an additional 70,000+ iPads to be used for state standardized testing (Blume, 2015). This iPad program, which was estimated to cost $1.3 billion, was plagued with problems stemming from the curriculum/content created for the program or the lack of availability of that content. Ultimately, the school district "reached a tentative $6.4-million settlement over curriculum from education software giant Pearson that the school system said its teachers barely used" (Blume, 2015, ¶. 1). We use this example to point out that even a device like the iPad, designed by Apple and one of the leading devices in the tablet market, by itself cannot sustain educational initiatives. Indeed, it appears that the issue with the L.A. iPad program had more to do with the availability of educational content than the iPads themselves. To truly use technology to help improve learning requires a deep integration of content and pedagogy; however, this may be more of the exception than the rule. We often find that technology is haphazardly introduced in the curriculum or that students are bringing their devices to class and attempting to use them for learning. In this chapter, we explore three ways in which students are using devices in the classroom (mobile phones, notebook computers, and e-books) and discuss how research has examined student learning in these areas.

Initial Research

Our initial work, that lead to examining the effects of mobile devices in class on student learning, started as a discussion in a graduate seminar at Ohio University (OU). That seminar examined instructional communication and we were spending a couple class sessions discussing technology in the classroom. Many of the doctoral students in that class also had assistantships and taught a variety of classes at OU. The class conversation shifted from the readings that day to how, as instructors, we could use technology in the classroom, as well as how our students were using technology. One general theme began to emerge and that was a variety of different instructors, teaching different classes, noted that they were seeing more and more students using their mobile phones in class. The generally consensus was that those students were likely texting or checking social media or social networking sites during class. As the conversation unfolded, the graduate students could be divided into two camps: one viewed this usage as unlikely to affect their learning (i.e., students could listen and use their devices at the same time) and the other view was that students using their mobile phones were distracting themselves from the classroom and likely wouldn't remember much from the class. Eventually, the conversation shifted back to our readings when a student asked what the current literature had to say about this behavior. At that time, early 2011, much of the research focused on notebook computers. For example, Kraushaar and Novak (2010) looked at student multitasking on laptops during class lecture and found that students often used software for non-course-related purposes and students also tended to underreport that usage. Around that time, other scholars were looking at texting behaviors in the classroom. For example, Wei, Wang, and Klausner (2012) examined student self-regulation and how texting during class may affect perceived cognitive learning. In addition, Campbell (2006) wrote an early study that examined perceptions of mobile phones in the classroom. However, much of the existing literature at the time, at least in the communication discipline, was not able to answer a specific question: how does mobile phone use in class affect student grades? That simple question began our research examining student use of mobile devices in the college classroom. In particular, our initial research (Kuznekoff & Titsworth, 2013) used an experimental design to collect data, something that much of past research had not done. Our studies examined how student messaging in class, particularly during a class lecture, negatively impacted student learning, recall, and note-taking (important learning behaviors). Importantly, by using an experimental design, we were able to control the environment our study was taking place in and, arguably, more closely mirror how students would be using their devices in their actual classes. This design allowed us to examine differences in test score, recall of content, and quality of student notes between students who were or were not using their mobile device during a simulated class lecture.

Mobile Phones in Class

For our experiment, we developed a 12-minute video lecture that all participants would watch. Beyond the lecture, we developed three different groups and manipulated how they used, or didn't use, their mobile device in each group. Our control group was told to put their mobile phones away and not to use them during the video lecture. The other students were told to take their phones out and, using an online system, those students were presented with simulated text messages or Facebook posts that they were asked to respond to. All of those

12 Challenges to Student Learning

simulated messages were entirely unrelated to the content of the video lecture and mimicked students interacting with someone, through their mobile device, who was outside of the classroom. Students in this experimental condition were randomly assigned to either a high or low texting condition. Students in the high condition received a message every 30 seconds, while the low condition received a message every 60 seconds.

Initially, we were expecting to find some minor differences; however, or significant finding was that the students who were actively messaging, responding to a new message every 30 seconds, scored 13% points lower on a test of the lecture content than the students who weren't using their phones. In addition, the students actively using their phones recalled less information and took lower quality notes than the students who abstained from texting. Our study provided clear evidence that students engaged in frequent, non-course-related messaging performed far worse than their counterparts who weren't messaging.

Although our initial study helped to answer an important question for students and faculty, that study was fairly limited in nature. For instance, students only responded to messages, they didn't create an original message or take the initiative to send a message to someone else. In addition, all of the messages we used were entirely unrelated to the video lecture. Although the design of that 2013 study was helpful, it did not account for additional ways that faculty might ask students to use mobile devices in the classroom or fully account for how students might be using their devices. For example, faculty in large lecture classes may ask students to use student response apps or even Twitter to send questions to the faculty member. It also seems likely that students aren't just responding to messages they receive during class, they likely are also creating their own messages and potentially even creating messages that relate to the class content.

To examine this area further, we developed a second experimental study (Kuznekoff et al., 2015) that built upon the prior one by adding in two important variables: message creation and message content. We wanted to examine if there was a difference in learning between students simply responding to a message or students creating their own original message. In addition, we also wanted to see if the content of those messages, related to or unrelated to class content, would impact learning. Following the same procedure as the prior study, we recruited students and had them watch that same video lecture. When examining the analog for the initial three groups from

Reducing Student Attention, Recall, & Note-taking 13

the 2013 study, we found the same trend, that students frequently texting learned less, recalled less, and took lower quality notes than students not texting. But we also found that message content played a role too. Those students who were messaging about lecture content (i.e., messages relevant to the lecture) did not suffer from the same decreases in learning, even when they were responding to messages every 30 seconds. It turns out that those students responding to class relevant content did not differ from the control group in terms of scores on the test of student learning, recall of information from the lecture, or in terms of the quality of their notes. Instead, what we found was that students who were frequently composing or responding to messages that were unrelated to class content typically scored the lowest on our tests of student learning. It would seem that all three variables: message content (related to or unrelated to class content), message creation (responding to preexisting message or creating your own), and frequency (high or low distraction), are important factors in impacting student learning.

This finding also means that educators do have options. You can use mobile devices for course appropriate ways without negatively impacting student learning, particularly when students are responding to course-relevant content. However, that is easier said than done. How do educators integrate technology into their lesson plans so that students are appropriately using technology without making that technology come across as a gimmick? How do we build this connection in such a way that students view this integration as seamless and not as simply tacked on? These are important questions that we address in this book; however, answers to those questions will very well take years to uncover.

Laptops/Notebooks in Class

Next to mobile phones, laptop computers in the classroom is likely one of the most prevalent devices that student bring to class. In their widely cited work, Sana, Weston, and Cepeda (2013) examined student use of laptops in class, noting that it often hinders student performance and may even prove distracting for students adjacent to the laptop. One of the core aspects of their argument for why laptops can decrease student performance has to do with the limited mental resources available to students. Sana et al. note that "When the level of available attentional resources is less than what is required to complete two simultaneous tasks, performance decrements are experienced since both tasks are competing for the same limited resources"

14 *Challenges to Student Learning*

(2013, p. 24). In other words, when students try to accomplish two tasks at the same time, both task performance suffer due to the competing use of the same mental resources. In their experiment, Sana et al. (2013) report that the notes of multitaskers was of lower quality than students who were not multitasking, which is echoed in our own research as well (Kuznekoff et al., 2015; Kuznekoff & Titsworth, 2013). Sana et al. (2013) are hardly the only study that has examined this student behavior. Kraushaar and Novak (2010) also studied student multitasking on laptops during class and found that "the average student engages in frequent multitasking during class, generating more than 65 new active windows per lecture, with 62% of those windows being classified as distractive" (p. 249). Similar to these past studies, scholars examined off-task behaviors in real-time class lectures (Wood et al., 2012). Wood et al. report that "and distraction, regardless of number, resulted in poorer performance than the no distraction condition" (2012, p. 372). Beyond the distraction research, Mueller and Oppenheimer (2014) examined note-taking between students who took notes on a laptop and those who took notes by hand. One of the findings from that study is the tendency of students using a laptop to take verbatim notes. In other words, students would write down nearly exactly what the instructor was saying; however, this type of note-taking behavior appears to hurt learning. Instead of listening and thinking through what the instructor is saying, and considering how to encode that information into one's notes, verbatim notetakers simply write down everything they hear and do not fully process that content. This turns students into transcription machines and "participants using laptops were more inclined to take verbatim notes than participants who wrote longhand, thus hurting learning" (Mueller & Oppenheimer, 2014, p. 1166). Furthermore, the authors report that students who took notes via a laptop performed worse on tests later on, even after being allowed to review their notes. Mueller and Oppenheimer (2014) state:

> One might think that the detriments to encoding would be partially offset by the fact that verbatim transcription would leave a more complete record for external storage, which would allow for better studying from those notes. However, we found the opposite—even when allowed to review notes after a week's delay, participants who had taken notes with laptops performed worse on tests of both factual content and conceptual understanding, relative to participants who had taken notes longhand.
>
> (p. 1166)

This study, and others, provide evidence that laptops in class, even when used for the purpose of taking notes, can be detrimental to student learning. Just as concerning, Mueller and Oppenheimer (2014) also report that even telling students to avoid taking verbatim notes was not enough to prevent that behavior from happening.

Technology in the Classroom

How do we, as educators, use technology in our classrooms to help our students and enhance their learning? This is a rather vexing question and one that we, as seasoned teachers and scholars, do not have a specific answer to. However, we do offer the following as a tentative discussion point. Any technology used in the classroom will likely fail, unless the use of that technology has been carefully considered from a pedagogical standpoint and directly tied with student learning outcomes. By itself, integrating technology without this careful consideration likely leads to disappointing results. We would argue that one example of this is the multiuser virtual environment Second Life, which was heralded as one of the next big things in higher education. Lagorio noted that "Scores of colleges and universities have set up campuses on islands, where classes meet and students interact in real time. They can hold chat discussions and create multimedia presentations from virtual building blocks called prims" (2007, ¶. 4). Many expected Second Life to open the doors to online learning by allowing faculty and students to interact in a vivid virtual environment. In fact, some identified Second Life as *the* platform of choice for higher education. Warburton (2009) noted that "the relatively low cost of entry, the ability to create complex objects and environments, combined with the sophistication of its graphics and the rich immersive experience, that are identified as establishing SL as the most attractive proposition for educators" (p. 418). However, Second Life failed to gain mass adoption and, in hindsight, appears to be a failed experiment with some virtual college campuses remaining as ghost towns. Hogan (2015) even took a tour of these abandoned virtual campuses, and Young (2016) notes that some educators may use the lessons learned from Second Life as they move to integrating virtual reality into the classroom. However, we would argue that without careful consideration, any use of technology in the classroom will likely fail unless it fulfills some sort of pedagogical need. In our experience, Second Life didn't meet this basic need. For example, when teaching quantitative research methods, we often teach students how to use software applications that conduct statistical analyses or online

16   *Challenges to Student Learning*

systems that can be used to design surveys and collect responses. The specific software application doesn't matter too much, instead it is using appropriate technology to help students actively engage in course concepts and, hopefully, to learn from that engagement. In the case of Second Life, the technology likely didn't meet a pressing classroom need and this likely became apparent to students fairly quickly. In their meta-analysis, Inman, Wright, and Hartman (2010) note that the problems with Second Life as an education tool include "technical problems, a steep learning curve, the potential for distraction and disruption caused by avatars unrelated to the class, and potential exposure to misinformation and pornography" (p. 56). Indeed, these are important problems, but the likely overarching issue is that Second Life didn't fulfill a pedagogical need. We would advocate that any educator exercise caution when integrating a new technology into their curriculum. In particular, it is likely best to avoid the novelty of the latest and greatest new app and, instead, to think carefully about what educational need is accomplished through that technology and, just as important, how will students use this technology in their education?

References

Blume, H. (2015, April 16). *L.A. school district demands iPad refund from Apple.* Retrieved from https://www.latimes.com/local/lanow/la-me-ln-ipad-curriculum-refund-20150415-story.html

Campbell, S. W. (2006). Perceptions of mobile phones in college classrooms: Ringing, cheating, and classroom policies. *Communication Education, 55*, 280–294. doi:10.1080/03634520600748573

Hogan, P. (2015, August 13). *We took a tour of the abandoned college campuses of Second Life.* Retrieved from https://splinternews.com/we-took-a-tour-of-the-abandoned-college-campuses-of-sec-1793849944

Inman, C., Wright, V. H., & Hartman, J. A. (2010). Use of Second Life in K-12 and higher education: A review of research. *Journal of Interactive Online Learning, 9*, 44–63.

Kraushaar, J. M., & Novak, D. C. (2010). Examining the affects of student multitasking with laptops during the lecture. *Journal of Information Systems Education, 21*, 241–251.

Kuznekoff, J. H., Munz, S. M., & Titsworth, B. S. (2015). Mobile phones in the classroom: Examining the effects of texting, Twitter, and message content on student learning. *Communication Education, 64*, 344–365. doi:10.1080/03634523.2015.1038727

Kuznekoff, J. H., & Titsworth, B. S. (2013). The impact of mobile phone usage on student learning. *Communication Education, 62*, 233–252. doi:10.1080/03634523.2013.767917

Reducing Student Attention, Recall, & Note-taking   17

Lagorio, C. (2007, January 7). *The ultimate distance learning.* Retrieved from https://www.nytimes.com/2007/01/07/education/edlife/07innovation.html

Mueller, P. A., & Oppenheimer, D. M. (2014). The pen is mightier than the keyboard: Advantages of longhand over laptop note taking. *Psychological Science, 25,* 1159–1168. doi:10.1177/0956797614524581

Sana, F., Weston, T., & Cepeda, N. J. (2013). Laptop multitasking hinders classroom learning for both users and nearby peers. *Computers & Education, 62,* 24–31. doi:10.1016/j.compedu. 2012.10.003

Warburton, S. (2009). Second Life in higher education: Assessing the potential for and the barriers to deploying virtual worlds in learning and teaching. *British Journal of Educational Technology, 40,* 414–426. doi:10.1111/j.1467–8535.2009.00952.x

Wei, F. F., Wang, Y. K., & Klausner, M. (2012). Rethinking college students' self-regulation and sustained attention: Does text messaging during class influence cognitive learning? *Communication Education, 61,* 185–204. doi:10.1080/03634523.2012.672755

Wood, E., Zivcakova, L., Gentile, P., Archer, K., De Pasquale, D., & Nosko, A. (2012). Examining the impact of off-task multi-tasking with technology on real-time classroom learning. *Computers & Education, 58,* 365–374.

Young, J. R. (2016, June 2). *Remember Second Life? Its fans hope to bring VR back to the classroom.* Retrieved from https://www.chronicle.com/article/Remember-Second-Life-Its-Fans/236675

3 Problematizing the "Digital Native"

Introduction

The primary focus of this chapter is a discussion of the term "digital native." This term has often been used to describe millennial students; however, it encompasses the traditional college student demographic. More recently, scholars have problematized this term as it oversimplifies a complex skill set that is not universally developed among college students. This chapter provides background information on the term "digital native" and a discussion of why instructors should avoid looking at competence with technology as a generational construct.

What Is a Digital Native

Shortly after the new millennium hit, a new term was coined and quickly entered the public lexicon, particularly when referring to young people, college students, and millennials. That term, the "digital native", has persisted over time and continues to be used to explain not just millennials but also the generation that follows. Prensky (2001) is typically credited with coining this term, and it is used to describe students, generally born in the mid-1980s, who have grown up with and are immersed in technology. According to Prensky, these students "*think and process information fundamentally differently from their predecessors*" (p. 1). The argument then becomes that because technology was such a key component in their lives, students of this generation are technology literature, adept at using technology, and prefer technology over previous ways of doing things, including education. Brown and Czerniewicz (2010) explain that "the leap is then made that students are therefore all technically proficient using a range of these technology, and that 'they do things differently'" (p. 357). This assumption, that students are all proficient with a range

Problematizing the "Digital Native" 19

of technologies, is one that has been widely circulated. Prensky (2001) goes on to note that digital natives are:

> used to receiving information really fast. They like to parallel process and multi-task. They prefer their graphics before their text rather than the opposite. They prefer random access (like hypertext). They function best when networked. They thrive on instant gratification and frequent rewards. They prefer games to "serious" work.
>
> (p. 2)

Those who are not digital natives may be considered digital immigrants, and Prensky proposes that many college-level instructors fall within this term. According to his definition, digital immigrants are "Those of us who were not born into the digital world but have, at some later point in our lives, become fascinated by and adopted many or most aspects of the new technology" (Prensky, 2001, pp. 1–2). Nearly a decade later, he further explains that "So to me, being a Digital Native is about growing up in a digital country or culture, as opposed to coming to it as an adult" (Prensky, 2011, p. 17). However, the way in which we think about digital natives and millennial students, that they easily adapt to and use technology, is problematic for a number of reasons, and challenging this assumption is something that a variety of scholars have done. Indeed, Jones (2011) notes that the term "digital native" and the accompanying explanation has persisted over time and, as with other ideas, has proven "highly resistant to refutation" (p. 41).

Problematizing the Digital Native

Kirschner and De Bruyckere (2017) challenge the notion of the digital native, noting "many teachers, educational administrators, and politicians/policy makers believe in the existence of yeti-like creatures populating present day schools namely *digital natives* and *human multitaskers*" (p. 135). However, these international scholars note that evidence supporting the widely held belief of digital natives being technological experts is often lacking. For example, they cite a variety of studies, from different countries, that give us pause when considering the validity of our assumptions concerning digital natives. Kirschner and De Bruyckere note that when examining students born after 1984 (i.e., within the definition of millennial), researchers have found that these students "do not have deep knowledge of technology,

20   Challenges to Student Learning

and what knowledge they do have is often limited to the possibilities and use of basic office suite skills, emailing, text messaging, Facebook®, and surfing the Internet" (p. 136). In particular to education, Prensky (2001) notes that "today's learners are *different*" (p. 3) and, as a result of this difference, education practices and systems need to change to better teach this group. However, researchers have also provided evidence to challenge this notion as well. Margaryan, Littlejohn, and Vojt (2011) found:

> Our study showed that far from demanding lecturers change their practice, students appear to conform to fairly traditional pedagogies, albeit with minor uses of technology tools that deliver content. In fact students' emphasised that they expected to be "taught" in traditional ways. On this basis, previous claims of a growing and uniform generation of young students entering higher education with radically different expectations about how they will learn seem unwarranted.
>
> (p. 438)

These scholars also note that a variety of studies, from different countries, are beginning to reach a similar conclusion, specifically that the term "digital native" is overly simplistic in explaining how students use technology (Margaryan et al., 2011).

For example, Brown and Czerniewicz (2010) report on a six-year research project in higher education institutions in South Africa, specifically examining students' access to connected devices. They note that, although age is proposed as a feature of being a digital native, they did not find evidence of the proposed connection between age and digital literacy. Within their study setting of South Africa, Brown and Czerniewicz (2010) report:

> students born into the millennial generation cannot be assumed to have grown up digital, nor can homogeneity be assumed in terms of computer experience. Rather, it is evident that the range of skills and experience of the students within "the millennial generation" is diverse.
>
> (p. 360)

These authors go on to note that only a small percentage of millennial students met Prensky's (2001) proposed definition and rather than being viewed as a homogeneous description of a generation of students, it is better to view the concept of a digital native as being more of a

Problematizing the "Digital Native" 21

range of skill sets or as a continuum. In addition, Brown and Czerniewicz (2010) also note that social advantage or disadvantage comes into play. While this may vary by country, socioeconomic status is related to access to newer digital devices.

Other approaches to examining this area have also discovered similar findings. Thomas' (2011) book examines the term "digital natives" from a variety of different perspectives. In another book, boyd (2014) discusses themes that emerged through her interviews with 166 teens across the United States. In particular, the theme of literacy and the question of are today's young people truly digital natives is an important consideration to make. In summarizing the notion of digital literacy and digital native, boyd explains:

> We live in a technologically mediated world. Being comfortable using technology is increasingly important for everyday activities: obtaining a well-paying job, managing medical care, engaging with government. Rather than assuming that youth have innate technical skills, parents, educators, and policymakers must collectively work to support those who come from different backgrounds and have different experiences. Educators have an important role to play in helping youth navigate networked publics and the information-rich environments that the internet supports. Familiarity with the latest gadgets or services is often less important than possessing the critical knowledge to engage productively with networked situations, including the ability to control how personal information flows and how to look for and interpret accessible information.
>
> (p. 180)

Similar to other findings (i.e., Brown & Czerniewicz, 2010; Margaryan et al., 2011), the assumption stemming from Prensky (2001), that young people or millennials have grown up with technology and therefore are adept at using it, does not appear to be accurate and this assumption has shifted the discussion of education.

Checking Our Assumptions

We tend to think that millennials prefer online and heavily mediated classrooms. In fact, several studies have challenged this notion that entering students need to be taught differently or enter school with radically different expectations. For instance, Lai and Hong (2015) report that "although the younger generation of students may

22 Challenges to Student Learning

do things and learn slightly differently, their way of using digital technology is similar to older generations of learners" (p. 736). In addition, these authors note that although students certainly do use digital technology, that usage is more complex than it has been explained by others.

For example, Smith (2014) reports that younger Internet users appear to be slightly more knowledgeable than older users when it comes to general web knowledge; however, "these differences are most pronounced on the questions dealing with social media, as well as common internet usage conventions" (p. 3). In a small-scale study, Nicholas (2008) asked students about different class study methods and if the students agreed or disagreed that those methods helped them better understand a class topic. Within that study, 92% agreed that handwritten notes in class helped them, while only 52% agreed that typing notes in class helped them. In addition, less than 22% of students indicated that listening to recorded lectures helped them and 78% disagreed with that statement. Lastly, nearly 63% of participants noted that they preferred lecture as a format of class instruction.

While citing a few studies is far from demonstrating a significant trend, we would offer that the inclination to identifying today's college students as so different from past students that instructors must radically transform their teaching practice as being an overdramatization. Most certainly, students and technology have changed, and so has higher education. However, we would caution against assuming that every aspect of higher education must be embedded with technology. Instead, we view technology as a tool that, when used carefully and appropriately, can be a powerful learning tool that enables students to learn.

Moving Forward

In order to have an informed conversation about how to and if to integrate technology into learning, we need to dispel these past assumptions. We should view technology competence on a continuum and recognize that millennials and entering college students are not entering college and universities as experts in technology. Instead, we need to recognize that young people have a complex relationship with technology and digital devices, and this relationship is not homogeneous in nature. As educators, we are well situated to explore and critique the way in which technology can positively and negatively affect student learning, and later chapters of this book take up that call.

References

boyd, d. (2014). *It's complicated: The social lives of networked teens.* New Haven, CT: Yale University Press.

Brown, C., & Czerniewicz, L. (2010). Debunking the "digital native": Beyond digital apartheid, towards digital democracy. *Journal of Computer Assisted Learning, 26*, 357–369. doi:10.1111/j.1365-2729.2010.00369.x

Jones, C. (2011). Students, the net generation, and digital natives. In M. Thomas (Ed.), *Deconstructing digital natives: Young people, technology and the new literacies* (pp. 30–45). New York, NY: Routledge.

Kirschner, P. A., & De Bruyckere, P. (2017). The myths of the digital native and the multitasker. *Teaching and Teacher Education, 67*, 135–142. doi:10.1016/j.tate.2017.06.001

Lai, K., & Hong, K. (2015). Technology use and learning characteristics of students in higher education: Do generational differences exist? *British Journal of Educational Technology, 46*(4), 725–738. doi:10.1111/bjet.12161

Margaryan, A., Littlejohn, A., & Vojt, G. (2011). Are digital natives a myth or reality? University students' use of digital technologies. *Computers & Education, 56*, 429–440. doi:10.1016/j.compedu.2010.09.004

Nicholas, A. (2008). *Preferred learning methods of the millennial generation.* Retrieved from https://digitalcommons.salve.edu/

Prensky, M. (2001). Digital natives, digital immigrants part 1. *On the Horizon, 9*(5), 1–6. doi:10.1108/10748120110424816

Prensky, M. (2011). Digital wisdom and homo sapiens digital. In M. Thomas (Ed.), *Deconstructing digital natives: Young people, technology and the new literacies* (pp. 15–29). New York, NY: Routledge.

Smith, A. (2014). *What internet users know about technology and the web: The Pew Research Center's "web iq" quiz.* Retrieved from http://www.pewresearch.org

Thomas, M. (Ed.). (2011). *Deconstructing digital natives: Young people, technology and the new literacies.* New York, NY: Routledge.

4 Digital Inequality and Digital Literacy Skills

Introduction

Moving beyond traditional inquiries related to access and adoption of technology, this chapter examines how digital inequality influences a student's educational experience in the university classroom. Often students who belong to minoritized communities, lower socioeconomic classes, or live in rural spaces experience a multidimensional inequality of digital access and connectivity. Frequently, the digital divide is denoted as the gap in society between those with access to and knowledge of modern technology; however, this understanding fails to recognize the disparities that exist with connectivity and technological devices. Although traditional age college students do use technology quite frequently, it would be a mistake to assume that all students have access to and are proficient in using specific technologies. Students who enter the university classroom with the privileges of the latest mobile devices and access to reliable broadband high-speed internet often have more developed digital literacy skills, which often take years to develop and put into practice.

While technology and access have increased in diffusion, students who enter the university classroom from digital divide backgrounds are faced with the challenges of weaker digital skills, which are essential for mobilizing educational resources. Problematizing this further, even if students do have access to a smartphone, the brand and capabilities of that phone can vary widely. With all technologies, the hardware, software, and skills necessary to operate them may vary in different ways. For instance, the iPhone X (which costs roughly $1,000) is a more robust and powerful device than a $30 Android touchscreen phone. While both are "smartphones," they are capable of doing very different tasks and thus device fragmentation may limit students' ability to accomplish digital tasks.

Digital Inequality and Digital Literacy Skills   25

This chapter will interrogate these important issues and challenge the assumptions the scholarly community often makes about students and technology. Beginning, first by contextualizing the term _digital divide._ Then, moving to a discussion of understanding digital inequality and digital literacy skills as they intersect with social identity experiences in the university classroom. Each section offers knowledge claims derived from research as well as affords some practical suggestions for technology use in the classroom.

The Digital Divide

The term, _digital divide_, suggests that there is a division between two so-called groups in society. In short, the digital divide is used to oversimplify the complex and abstract issue of access, maintenance, and technology use in society. Rather a more appropriate term, _digital differentiation,_ suggests that the digital divide is a dynamic phenomenon influenced by social identity experiences and political-cultural resources (Van Dijk, 2012). Illustrating this more complex understanding, the contemporary digital divide in the U.S. encompasses, but is not limited to, people's experiences with "struggling to maintain physical access" to an internet connection (Gonzales, 2016, p. 234). Ongoing disparities in physical access for the U.S. poor as well as those living in rural communities means users may experience frequent periods of internet disconnections, recurrently broken hardware, or disproportionally high monthly payments due to limited internet providers (Gonzales, 2016). In this way, the digital divide may not only entail physical access but also intersect with ongoing social inequalities. Another complexity identified by Gonzales (2014) is how mobile devices offer psychological reassurance for individuals living in poor U.S. urban communities. Although the devices were often second-hand or no-contract phones, participants reported feelings of extreme reassurance in the possibility of being able to report crimes and reduce recidivism in their communities. Taken together, we argue that it is more appropriate to place the digital divide alongside other social inequalities as it affects participation in the labor force, civic life, and academic performance.

Another worthy consideration regarding the digital divide is that theoretically and through application, it has predominately focused on examining adult users' information seeking behaviors, thereby ignoring adolescent users. Understanding young people's technology motivations and information skills may elucidate differential use patterns in the university classroom. Beginning to address this concern,

26 Challenges to Student Learning

Robinson (2014) argues that we may know less about adolescent students because of the beliefs surrounding youths as "wired" which fails to address segments of the population that are "partially wired Internet users" with varied information seeking skills (p. 236). Robinson's (2014) research forwards that students who lack learning opportunities at home, lack information seeking and evaluation skills in school. Further, Robinson (2014) found that unskilled female students will overtrust, while male students will undertrust internet information as factually accurate. These findings present a more nuanced understanding of youth's experiences with technology.

As we consider the experiences of adolescents' information seeking and evaluative skills, it is worthwhile to also take into account how digital differentiation intersects with parent-teacher communication preferences. Similar to how the university classroom has shifted and adapted to integrate technology, so too, has P-12 classroom education and parent-teacher communication. Widely accepted as one of the most influential aspects of P-12 students' academic success, parent support can be represented through face-to-face, phone, paper, and now includes computer-mediated communication (CMC) with teachers (Thompson & Mazer, 2012). The proliferation and access of mobile devices, Thompson, Mazar, and Grady (2015) explains, has shifted "parents' preference for frequent e-email communication" (Thompson et al., 2015, p. 187). Further, their findings suggest an emerging interest by parents and teachers to use text messaging to communicate about a student's academic experiences. If mobile devices can be used as a bridge to increase parent involvement, from a once a year face-to-face meeting to weekly emails, it is also possible to provide more consistent as well as increased academic support to P-12 students. For parents and guardians living at or below the poverty line, who may work for an hourly wage and are unable to take time off work, CMC via a mobile device helps to include them in their children's education.

There are individuals who have broadband connectivity and others who have dial-up; both groups have access, but the type of access is differentiated (Van Dijk, 2005). In examining smartphones, we also realize that there is a potential divide based on the types of smartphones individuals have, but also as a result of this, there is another divide based on the potential literacy skills developed. While the latest mobile device maybe a status symbol in communities living at or below the poverty, the reality is that unlike middle class or above socioeconomic communities, a smartphone is likely the only way young people can access the internet (Cohen, 2016). For students, needing to complete school assignments, this may mean completing the work on

Digital Inequality and Digital Literacy Skills 27

their phone; however, it is more likely these students will use a public library's computer and broadband connection. As Cohen (2016) suggests, there is "so much left to do to bridge the digital divide, but mobile device availability is one bright spot" (para. 15). In this way, we realize that the digital divide is more multilayered with many stratifications. Further, the digital divide is often misunderstood as a static divide, and we argue that it should be understood as multilayered, complex, and often murky differentiation between and among groups in society (see Dijk, 2005; Helsper, 2012; Katz & Gonzalez, 2016).

In discussions of the so-called digital divide, we are also remiss if we fail to recognize the production gap between consumers and producers of knowledge. By embracing an understanding of the digital divide as evolving, we recognize that today, there remain questions about people's use of the internet, internet consumption, and how people use the internet to produce content (Stern, Adams, & Elsasser, 2009). Scholars have recognized that the digital divide is about more than providing necessary technological tools, but that individuals may require knowledge and training to use the resources (Kvasny, 2006; Stern et al., 2009). Another important concern with the term "digital divide" is that it has long evacuated individuals' identity (race, ethnicity, gender) from understanding digital experiences. In this way, individuals were homogenized into groups of either having or not having internet access, rather than clusters based on similar cultural identity and experiences. So, what exactly does digital inequality look like?

Digital Inequality and Digital Literacy

By considering and accepting the digital divide as complex, we then start from a place of realizing digital inequality is more or equally complex. Digital inequality is more than the "haves" and "the have nots" of technology resources or internet access. It includes not only those individuals, but also others who are dropouts, momentarily or permanently disconnected from the internet, but also individuals with outdated, used devices, and unreliable internet access. In short, digital inequality refers to disparities in access (internet/devices), proficiency of use, or differences in motivations which influence knowledge and frequency of use. Fully appreciating the relationship between digital inequality and other forms of inequality, Robinson et al. (2015) argue "digital inequality deserves a place alongside more traditional forms of inequality in the twenty-first century" (p. 570). In this way, we begin to consider how digital inequality maybe connected to not only other forms of inequality but also the broad range of implications,

28 Challenges to Student Learning

outcomes, and consequences as they connect to educational experiences. The following section summarizes current research on digital inequality as it relates to a life course perspective, socioeconomic, race, and ethnicity, as well as gender identity experiences. Finally, implications for student learning in the university classroom are also interrogated.

Life Course

Within the literature, a life course approach helps to outline how through different life realms digital inequality exists, disappears, or re-emerges. In short, a life course perspective refers to examining people's lives through cultural, structural, political, and social contexts (Robinson, Chen, Schulz, & Khilnani, 2018). According to Robinson, Wiborg, and Shultz (2018), digital inequalities during adolescence may disadvantage individuals into adulthood and negatively influence academic achievement in the classroom. These findings indicate that for students entering the university classroom from backgrounds of digital inequality may experience significant academic disadvantages in successfully participating in online assignments. As the university classroom continues to become a space of near compulsory technology requirement, these students may experience academic disadvantages both in the online and face-to-face room, as the later becomes increasingly reliant on electronic submission of assignments, activities, and resources. For adult learners in the twenty-first-century university classroom, they are likely to experience moments of digital uncertainty and even isolation but may acquire social support from experts and peers (Robinson, Chen, et al., 2018). For educators, it is important to keep the myriad of benefits afforded by technology as well as the stress, challenges, and disadvantages in mind, too.

Socioeconomic

While levels of access to cell phones, computers, tablets, and the internet appear to have reached high levels of saturation in the undergraduate populations, inequalities as result of economic inequalities still exist (Robinson et al., 2015). Cultural scholars have argued that socioeconomic status begins to impact type of internet access and production of information for individuals at a young age and frequently persists though adulthood (Peter & Valkenburg, 2006).

For students, factors such as computer and cell phone age, internet speed, and device reliability and quality all influence their ability to be

Digital Inequality and Digital Literacy Skills 29

successful students in the classroom. For students belonging to lower socioeconomic statuses, Gonzales (2016) posits that they are more likely to have limited functioning resources because they are unable to afford "maintenance costs" associated with technology (p. 243). Students belonging to lower socioeconomic communities are also more likely to face quality and connection issues in comparison to the peers belonging to middle and upper classes. In the age of flipped classrooms, online and hybrid courses, ready and reliable access to the internet is arguably a necessity for academic success.

A prevalent complication for students belonging to lower socioeconomic classes, perhaps as a result of unstable, unreliable, or infrequent use of technology is that they are often less likely to have positive feelings toward technology (Gonzales, 2016). Because of these feelings they maybe more likely to go without the internet as well as use it far less than they choose to because the quality is unstable or reliable. Related to availability of the internet, it is also important to consider how rural, suburban, and urban places may all differ in the infrastructure that facilitates internet access (for a full discussion of place-based internet inequalities, see Stern et al., 2009). For low-income users, they often hold weaker ties to the internet which can translate into weaker social networking, search engine, and web browsing skills. Scholars continue to speculate about whether or not it is because of quality or usability of technology resources, limited time to spend developing tech-skills, as well as lack of money to support technology (see Dijk, 2005; Gonzales, 2016).

In fact, low-income users of technology face ongoing issues as digital diffusion continues in the United States. For example, Powell, Bryne, and Dailey (2010) found that low-income users were often "piecing together strategies of Internet" (e.g., outdated phone with high-speed internet or broken technology with new accessory parts to increase functionality) (Powell et al., 2010, p. 181). If a student is unable to access a stable and reliable internet connection, s/he may try to use on campus or public library computers. However, often students from low socioeconomic backgrounds face access barriers in these spaces too because the computers maybe broken; the computers and internet access may have time limits; or there are not enough machines, and demand is high so s/he is unable to access a computer. For students, these types of experiences negatively impact their ability to successfully complete academic assignments and may also undermine their sense of self-efficacy. While smartphones have helped bridge socioeconomic gaps, the gap nevertheless persists and disproportionally disadvantages Black and Hispanic Americans as well as low-income

30　*Challenges to Student Learning*

households (Pew Research Center, 2015). The experiences of individuals from minoritized racial and ethnic backgrounds merit attention and scrutiny.

Race and Ethnicity

When we examine individual predicators of digital inequality, it is critical to understand how different racial and ethnic groups access and engage with digital technologies. As racial and ethnic minoritized groups hold different positionalities within U.S. and global society, their access and engagement is also differentiated and stratified. This is particularly important considering previous research has established that social inequalities for members of minoritized racial and ethnic groups are replicated in digital spaces (Robinson et al., 2015). This may mean smaller online networks and greater network homophily (or higher concentrations of similar others). Contextualizing this in the student context, this may result in a smaller network of members who also have limited access, skills, or digital resources in comparison to individuals with a diverse network. For students, inadequate access to the internet and/or digital devices may impact their academic success; however, for minoritized students, their academic experience maybe further complicated by an absence of a network with technological knowledge and access. Contributing to the complexity of understanding digital inequality, Robinson et al. (2018) assert that U.S. Latinos and African Americans self-report higher levels of online content creation in comparison to U.S. Whites. In fact, African Americans outpace White users in terms of online content creation (Robinson et al., 2015). Such findings are a call for further investigation into the role of online content creation in mitigating digital inequalities.

In large part, research has primarily focused on individual-level predicators of digital inequality; however, it is important to see these as intersectional rather than singular and isolated from one another. Simoni et al. (2016) argue for addressing the implications digital inequality with racial identity and living space. In their research, Simoni et al. (2016) assert that neighborhoods with a higher percentage of Black residents are less likely to use computers, which supports previous research that racial makeup in spaces (or neighborhoods) may reinforce technology inequalities. Other researchers have also established that neighborhood-level education and income level among minorities were predictors of technology use (see Mossberger, Tolbert, & Gilbert, 2006). Put another way, the higher the income level, the more likely individuals were to use technology, which

Digital Inequality and Digital Literacy Skills 31

may help perpetuate the status quo. Further, adding explanation to patterns of unequal access, scholars assert that Latino and Black students are often less likely to report having computer or internet access or the skills to use either, despite having positive attitudes toward technology (Mossberger et al., 2006).

An even more complex picture is realized, when we consider how race, ethnicity, and income level influence digital inequality and achievement. For students, from low-income, racial, and/or ethnic minoritized backgrounds they are likely to collide with a "digital bind" or an environment where digital resources are required for educational work, but neither the school nor their home can assure access (Robinson, Chen, et al., 2018, p. 1254). Such experiences may negatively influence students' educational experiences not only in the short term as they may fall behind in foundational skill development but also in the long-term cumulative developmental processes as well as in the motivating factors (Robinson et al., 2018).

Gender

Today, research on the digital gender gap focuses on the underlying mechanisms that cause digital inequality as well as the consequences as a result. While the gap between women and men accessing technology in the U.S. has narrowed, this does not hold true with respect to how individuals utilize technology or the internet (Blank & Groselj, 2014). For example, Cotton and Jelenewicz (2006) forward that women are more likely than men to utilize the internet for social support activities such as online chatting, networking building, or blogging activities. Supporting this, scholars have suggested that women in comparison to men are more likely to utilize technology for activities that help build relational networks and, therefore, more frequently utilize social networking sites (SNSs) when using the internet (Ertl & Helling, 2011). Such findings seem to be consistent with societal gender expectations for women; however, there are also forms of stereotyping which often fail to recognize motivational, affective, cognitive, as well as other identity and personality characteristics, in addition to environment and contextual complexities (Ertl & Helling, 2011).

While a collective agreement on the relationship between gender and internet use has yet to be solidified by scholars, we suggest that instructors in the classroom remain aware of gender stereotyping and its relationship to technology. While digital access maybe disappearing between men and women in the U.S., scholars have posited that

32 Challenges to Student Learning

women are more likely in comparison to men to underestimate their online and technology skills (Hargittai & Shafer, 2006). This holds true even when women do not differ from their male counterparts in actual digital skills (Hargittai & Shafer, 2006). Findings such as these suggest that digital inequality differences exist, but in a way more complicated than simply access or even use, and likely in a subtler form. In the classroom, this is a serious concern because it speaks to a female student's sense of self-efficacy, which carries with it implications for how she may approach goals and challenges and, in turn, influence academic motivation and achievements.

Concluding Thoughts

Although not an exhaustive examination of the varying individual identity markers that may contribute to digital inequality, we are hopeful that this chapter affords educators a lens for examining the ongoing and evolving digital student experience. The reality of technology in the classroom learning space is quite simple: In some form, it is a permanent fixture in our classroom, fraught with the complexity of access and skill issues, as well as the implications of societal inequality. Today, the everyday classroom is increasingly becoming a space where students are expected to access, utilize, and produce information via tablets, cell phones, or laptops. Often instructors expect students to utilize a combination of technological hardware, software programs, and course content knowledge to complete assignments. Not only are students expected to access e-textbooks, but s/he is also required to upload and submit typed assignments and record and upload digital videos.

References

Blank, G., & Groselj, D. (2014). Dimensions of internet use: Amount, variety, and types. *Information, Communication & Society, 17*(4), 417–435. doi:10.1080/1369118X.2014.889189

Cohen, D. (2016, April 15). It's not only rich teens that have smartphones. Retrieved May 9, 2019, from The Atlantic website: https://www.theatlantic.com/technology/archive/2016/04/not-only-rich-teens-have-cell-phones-digital-divide/478278/

Cotten, S. R., & Jelenewicz, S. M. (2006). A disappearing digital divide among college students?: Peeling away the layers of the digital divide. *Social Science Computer Review, 24*(4), 497–506. https://doi.org/10.1177/0894439306286852

Digital Inequality and Digital Literacy Skills   33

Ertl, B., & Helling, K. (2011). Promoting gender equality in digital literacy. *Journal of Educational Computing Research, 45*(4), 477–503.

Gonzales, A. L. (2014). Health benefits and barriers to cell phone use in low-income urban U.S. neighborhoods: Indications of technology maintenance. Mobile Media & Communication, 2(3), 233–248. https://doi.org/10.1177/2050157914530297

Gonzales, A. (2016). The contemporary US digital divide: From initial access to technology maintenance. *Information, Communication & Society, 19*(2), 234–248. doi:10.1080/1369118X.2015.1050438

Haight, M., Quan-Haase, A., & Corbett, B. A. (2014). Revisiting the digital divide in Canada: The impact of demographic factors on access to the internet, level of online activity, and social networking site usage. *Information, Communication & Society, 17*(4), 503–519. doi:10.1080/13691 18X.2014.891633

Hargittai, E., & Shafer, S. (2006). Differences in actual and perceived online skills: The role of gender*. *Social Science Quarterly, 87*(2), 432–448. doi:10.1111/j.1540-6237.2006.00389.x

Helsper, E. J. (2012). A corresponding fields model for the links between social and digital exclusion. *Communication Theory, 22*(4), 403–426. doi:10.1111/j.1468-2885.2012.01416.x

Katz, V. S., & Gonzalez, C. (2016). Toward meaningful connectivity: Using multilevel communication research to reframe digital inequality. *Journal of Communication, 66*(2), 236–249. doi:10.1111/jcom.12214

Kvasny, L. (2006). Cultural (re)production of digital inequality in a US community technology initiative. *Information, Communication & Society, 9*(2), 160–181. doi:10.1080/13691180600630740

Mossberger, K., Tolbert, C., & Gilbert, M. (2006). Race, place, and information technology. *Urban Affairs Review, 41*(5), 583–620. doi:10.1177/1078087405283511

Peter, J., & Valkenburg, P. M. (2006). Adolescents' internet use: Testing the "disappearing digital divide" versus the "emerging digital differentiation" approach. *Poetics, 34*(4), 293–305. doi:10.1016/j.poetic.2006.05.005

Pew Research Center. (2015, March 5). Digital differences across local communities. Retrieved September 11, 2018, from Pew Research Center's: Journalism & Media website: http://www.journalism.org/2015/03/05/digital-differences-across-local-communities/

Powell, A., Bryne, A., & Dailey, D. (2010). The essential internet: Digital exclusion in low-income American communities. *Policy & Internet, 2*(2), 161–192. doi:10.2202/1944-2866.1058

Robinson, L. (2014). Freeways, detours, and dead ends: Search journeys among disadvantaged youth. *New Media & Society, 16*(2), 234–251. doi:10.1177/1461444813481197

Robinson, L., Chen, W., Schulz, J., & Khilnani, A. (2018). Digital inequality across major life realms. *American Behavioral Scientist, 62*(9), 1159–1166. doi:10.1177/0002764218773800

34 Challenges to Student Learning

Robinson, L., Cotten, S. R., Ono, H., Quan-Haase, A., Mesch, G., Chen, W., ... Stern, M. J. (2015). Digital inequalities and why they matter. *Information, Communication & Society, 18*(5), 569–582. doi:10.1080/13691 18X.2015.1012532

Robinson, L., Wiborg, O., & Schulz, J. (2018). Interlocking inequalities: Digital stratification meets academic stratification. American Behavioral Scientist, 62(9), 1251–1272. doi:10.1177/0002764218773826

Simoni, Z. R., Gibson, P., Cotten, S. R., Stringer, K., & Coleman, L. O. (2016). Does place matter? The effects of concentrated poverty on the computer use of elementary students. *Journal of Urban Technology, 23*(3), 3–21. https://doi.org/10.1080/10630732.2015.1073901

Stern, M. J., Adams, A. E., & Elsasser, S. (2009). Digital inequality and place: The effects of technological diffusion on internet proficiency and usage across rural, suburban, and urban counties. *Sociological Inquiry, 79*(4), 391–417. doi:10.1111/j.1475-682X.2009.00302.x

Thompson, B. C., & Mazer, J. P. (2012). Development of the parental academic support scale: Frequency, importance, and modes of communication. *Communication Education, 61*(2), 131–160. doi:10.1080/0363452 3.2012.657207

Thompson, B. C., Mazer, J. P., & Grady, E. F. (2015). The changing nature of parent–teacher communication: Mode selection in the smartphone era. *Communication Education, 64*(2), 187–207. doi:10.1080/03634523.201 5.1014382

Van Dijk, J. (2005). *The deepening divide : Inequality in the information society.* Thousand Oaks, CA: SAGE Publications, Inc.

Van Dijk, A. G. M. (2012). The evolution of the digital divide. *Stand Alone,* 57–75. doi:10.3233/978-1-61499-057-4-57

Part 3

Technology in the Classroom

5 The Active Classroom

In her book *Bandwith Recovery*, Verschelden (2017) observed that students' cognitive resources needed for learning are severely degraded by forces external to the classroom. She argues that marginalization based on race, class, sexual orientation, gender identity, and other manifestations of difference all serve to create stress for students—stress that subsumes mental resources necessary for learning. Verschelden's observations are oriented toward systematic stressors resulting from larger, sociopolitical forces.

Of course, there are also various episodic stressors that can usurp mental capacity. This volume and others have argued that digital distractions cause students to have split attention, focus time, and mental resources away from learning and generally result in lower academic performance (see Berry & Westfall, 2015; Duncan, Hoekstra, & Wilcox, 2012). Recent research suggests that students potentially allow themselves to become distracted by their cell phones (and potentially other smart devices) because they perceive the class (or teacher) as boring (Bolkan & Griffin, 2017). Whether episodic or systemic, Verschelden's (2017) conclusions point to a problem facing instructors: Students' cognitive resources often divided and overextended, and in such instances, their ability to learn is compromised.

Instructors have few tools to combat systemic distractions. However, sentiment is growing to try and limit episodic distractions like cell phone use (see Lancaster, 2018). Given the amount of digital distraction present in most classrooms, one might presume that educators and institutions would employ policy restrictions (e.g., cell phone bans) or classroom designs (e.g., desks that would make hiding use of cell phone more difficult) to mitigate distraction. In fact, some teachers are taking matters into their own hands. As reported in a 2015 *CNET* article, a science teacher in Florida was suspended for a week when he activated a cell phone jammer in his classroom—the

38 *Technology in the Classroom*

jammer ultimately disrupted signals in a very wide geographic area (Matyszczyk, 2015), which is in violation of Federal Communications Commission (FCC, 2015) rules and federal law.

Despite that instance and the anecdotal sentiment that cell phones use should be discouraged, there are many more examples of educational institutions making classrooms digital and mobile friendly. New trends in classroom design are making learning spaces more conducive to Bring Your Own Device (BYOD) principles and promoting the use of ubiquitous technologies like cell phones and tablets to improve learning. Moreover, instructors are increasingly finding ways to leverage technology and applications to shift them from digital distractions to powerful learning tools.

In this chapter, we advance the argument that ubiquitous technology, like cell phones and other smart devices, is powerful opportunities for learning. Moreover, we suggest that using, rather than limiting, such technology use is important for meeting students where they are at, which Verschelden (2017) argues is essential for helping students feel comfortable in learning situations. In the following sections, we explore three projects, used by instructors in classes, that explicitly promote use of mobile technology to accomplish on-task learning. We conclude with a final section synthesizing our argument that such approaches have appeal in how they promote learning situations that capitalize on students' familiarity and comfort with mobile technology.

Turn It Gold

In fall of 2017, a faculty member and several students at Ohio University formed a campus affiliate of #turnitgold, a national philanthropic organization that raises awareness and research funding to combat childhood cancer (see http://turnitgold.org). During the month of September, which is National Childhood Cancer Awareness Month, the campus organization (#turnitgoldOU) created a communication campaign within the city of Athens and also organized several large events to raise awareness about childhood cancer and to also obtain donations for the national organization. Many of the students were both members of the student organization and also enrolled in a capstone course taught by Dr. Lynn Harter, the faculty member who brought #turnitgold to campus.

The awareness and fundraising campaign enacted by #turnitgoldOU was complex. During the first year of the organization (2017), over 20 local businesses agreed to place coin donation boxes

The Active Classroom 39

in their stores, a local printing company printed several presentation placards for use at events, and both Ohio University and Athens High School agreed to have various athletic events designated as #turnitgold games, where athletes wore #turnitgold materials (as possible) during the games. In the second year (2018), these same activities were expanded to include multiple athletic events at the university, Athens High, and neighboring Alexander High School. Because the national #turnitgold organization emphasizes athletic activism as a primary communication strategy, inclusion of these local athletic events was important because it allowed the local affiliate to be consistent with the national organization's strategy. In addition to Harter's students and those officially in the #turnitgoldOU organization, curriculum planners for Ohio University's first-year experience seminar integrated #turnitgold into project-based activities for over 3,000 first-year students each year. In total, the #turnitgoldOU affiliate has raised over $50,000 dollars, has engaged tens of thousands community members at multiple events (particularly athletic events), and has involved well over 7,000 students in some capacity. The work was substantial and the outcomes impressive.

Harter and #turnitgoldOU enacted principles of problem-based learning. They identified a clear project—supporting the efforts of the national #turnitgold organization—but had freedom to engage that project as they thought best. Although the specific strategy of athletic activism was maintained, they also had free license to take other steps to raise awareness and donations. In Harter's capstone course, one of the students' projects was to create visual public service announcements that could be used with donation boxes and, in larger formats, at events. Notably, most students did not have explicit training in digital media production because they were communication studies majors where such courses are not required.

The example in Figure 5.1 shows a public service announcement image created by Professor Harter and her students. The football game PSA used an image from the previous year, taken by the faculty member, to create artwork appropriate for display at the Ohio University #turnitgold game during the subsequent year. Using images taken with smartphones and basic Photoshop editing, such as adding text and other graphics, the faculty member and her students were able to employ readily available technology to enact their communication campaign. During class, Harter created this image with her students to illustrate what she expected of them as they produced other images. For example, all PSA artwork was required to have a fact or statistic about pediatric cancer integrated into the image.

40 *Technology in the Classroom*

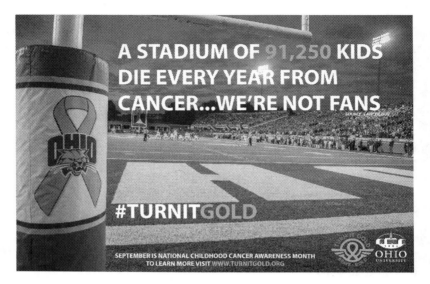

Figure 5.1 #turnitgold Game Public Service Message

A second example involved true problem-solving skills. In the public tweet about #turnitgold apparel, readers can observe that students were selling special t-shirts, wrist bands, and other #turnitgold merchandise. Initial slow sales caused some degree of frustration, but the reason was quickly obvious to the students—their peers do not carry cash. After some quick problem-solving among the students, they presented a plan to Dr. Harter to create a Venmo account for #turnitgoldOU. For other pre-millennials, we quickly learned that Venmo (and similar apps) are now primary ways that students purchase things, pay rent, etc. Once a #turnitgoldOU Venmo account was up and running, merchandise sales quickly boomed.

The PSA and Venmo examples illustrate how Harter and her students used mobile technology, or what we more generally call ubiquitous technology, as integral learning tools. Although students were not trained in visual communication principles or techniques, their experience with social media and available technologies allowed them to create PSAs that were targeted, well planned, and visually compelling. The Venmo solution leveraged their own technology knowledge as a solution to a critical problem for the organization. In this example, students were engaged by course concepts because their personal knowledge of mobile technology was a primary resource for the class rather than something to be banned or discouraged.

Active Learning Classrooms

In 2014, Ohio University completed a $38M renovation of facilities for the Scripps College of Communication. One space inside that building became a focal point for our vision of how ubiquitous technology could be incorporated into a modern educational facility. Initial plans for an approximately 130-seat classroom called for a very conventional lecture-style room with "horseshoe" placement of fixed tables and seats. In essence, the room was initially designed as a slightly more comfortable lecture hall.

Prior to the start of the project, Scott Titsworth, then Interim Dean of the college, engaged faculty to re-imagine the nature of that room. Because another large lecture hall existed in the building design, the need for another lecture-style classroom appeared, at best, circumspect. As final plans were developed by the architectural firm, we explored various alternatives to create a more engaging and innovative classroom.

Initial exploration of literature revealed a handful of universities that had created active learning classrooms (ALCs), primarily for STEM related fields. We discovered a website (http://scaleup.ncsu.edu) synthesizing both examples and research on ALCs across the country. In general, ALCs involve use of tables that facilitate group interaction (think round or "guitar pick"-shaped tables). These classrooms also typically have video monitors for each table that allow easy connection by students with laptops or other mobile technology; each table also typically has a whiteboard. Because these classrooms are explicitly designed for interaction rather than lecture, the ideal pedagogy used by faculty in the rooms tends to be problem and group-based rather than traditional lecture formats. Moreover, many faculty employ "flipped classroom" principles where students obtain content outside of class and then apply that content in some way while in class. Notably, these types of classrooms remain conducive to large sections. In our case, the Scripps College was able to redesign the classroom to seat 140 students, the same approximate number that would have fit into the traditional lecture-style configuration.

Since our exploration of ACLs in 2010, a growing body of research points to their efficacy for high-impact teaching and learning experiences. Gordy, Jones, and Bailey (2018) conducted a qualitative study using participant observation and interviews and found that ALC classes resulted in greater interaction between students and teachers, diminished hierarchy between students and teachers, substantial course engagement by students, greater integration of creativity, and improved collaboration among students as they completed

42 *Technology in the Classroom*

assignments and projects. A 2017 study by Hyun, Ediger, and Lee found that students report significantly higher levels of satisfaction in ALCs as compared to traditional classrooms. Research also shows that ALC students significantly outperform their peers in traditional classrooms on exams (Entezari & Javdan, 2016).

A notable feature of most ACLs is substantial access to technology (Nicol, Owens, Le Coze, Macintyre, & Eastwood, 2018). For example, in the Scripps College's ALC, each table has a 47″ monitor and 6′ whiteboard; students have the ability to wirelessly connect to the monitor or can use more conventional hardwired connections like HDMI. Faculty teaching in this room are able to display content on three projector screens placed throughout the room, including input from any of the 16 table monitors. Access to those resources is a key aspect of how instructors plan and execute daily lesson plans for classes assigned to the room.

We require faculty to undergo training in the semester prior to using the room and to also observe classes in the room prior to teaching in the space. As Nicol and colleagues (2018) noted, the robust technology package in such rooms magnify potential problems. We have found that user training not only reduces problems due to user error but also increases the likelihood that instructors can diagnose and resolve problems as they arise.

Specific applications of our ALC vary by instructor. One teacher actively uses twitter as a community note-taking space during class. Students tweet notable elements of each class period using a unique hashtag, which can later be reviewed by peers as they fill in notes and/or study for exams. Because the twitter feed is displayed throughout the room, the teacher can have real-time monitoring of what students are pulling from lecture or discussion. Students in our visual communication capstone courses work collaboratively to annually create an online multimedia storytelling project (see http://2018.soulofathens.com for example). Because the project involves nearly 50 students from multiple sub-specialties, the collaboration opportunities afforded by the ALC have been transformative. Other faculty, such as those teaching undergraduate research method courses use flipped classroom principles so that class time can focus on synthesis, analysis, and evaluation of statistical and qualitative methods in application. Students also use the technology to collaborate on team-based research projects as the semester unfolds.

Now nearly five years into having the ALC, we observe that the flexibility offered by the unique learning space has led to exciting new opportunities. Students in a club E-Sports team began using the classroom during evening hours in 2017. Now, that club team has grown to over 200 students and the university is actively pursuing a competitive intercollegiate E-Sports team that will be integrated into curricular offerings in multiple colleges. The appeal of our ALC for this use is that multiple groups can bring game consoles directly into the room, connect to monitors, and have the ability to play games in a collaborative space where spectators can easily view action on the large screens.

Both traditional uses of our ALC and emergent uses, such as E-Sports, have achieved success because the ALC is designed to actively accommodate ubiquitous technology. Students can easily use the room with nothing more than their phones but can also bring laptops, tablets, game consoles, and other devices and use them in a plug-and-play fashion. Based on the design of the room, we have found it to be a dynamic learning space that promotes innovative teaching and learning. Importantly, the technology does not drive learning *per se* but does facilitate an environment where everyday technology can be meaningfully integrated into learning.

Virtual and Augmented Reality

The 2016 Horizons Report for higher education (Johnson et al., 2016) identified augmented and virtual reality (AR/VR) as a key technology trend that would emerge within 2–3 years. Since that time, AR/VR technology has achieved that promise by disrupting training in fields ranging from medicine to art. As explained by Chandrasekera and Yoon (2018), consumer adoption has led to mainstream use of AR/VR and lowered barriers for adoption of the technology in educational settings.

AR/VR are distinct but closely related immersive experiences. VR immerses users into a completely virtual environment through carefully designed animated experiences or through 360° video. Users experience VR by wearing headsets that place wide-angle screens in front of their eyes and by using sound canceling earphones for audio. Through those devices, users are perceptually cut off from their physical environment, making the virtual environment highly realistic. Although early applications of VR technology had side effects, such as motion sickness, the technology has evolved to eliminate such problems. Facebook's Occulus Rift and Occulus Go headsets are examples of consumer-facing VR technologies.

AR does not isolate users from their physical environment. Using clear headsets (and in for some applications headphones), users view

44 *Technology in the Classroom*

animations and other information overlaid on clear lenses, allowing a virtual immersive experience to blend with an actual physical setting. Google glasses and Pokemon Go are examples of consumer-facing AR technology.

Both AR and VR have retained some barriers for widespread adoption. Typical application of both technologies requires investment in headsets for optimal user experiences. Headset options for AR/VR vary in price, but good options for both range from approximately $200–$400 for basic but robust systems. However, smartphones coupled with solutions like Google Cardboard—a cardboard headset that holds your smartphone in front of your eyes—can all but eliminate the price barrier for most consumers. Moreover, AR apps are rapidly expanding on smartphone and other mobile platforms. Thus, the financial entry barriers for using AR/VR technology are diminishing for those who do not require optimal or premium experiences.

Advances in technology coupled with diminished cost have accelerated adoption of AR/VR technology in education. Adoption of such technology has been documented in the humanities where teachers use immersive environments to create historical empathy (Sweeney, Newbill, Ogle, & Terry, 2018), in music education to improve conducting skills (Orman, Price, & Russell, 2017), and health sciences (Moro, Štromberga, Raikos, & Sterling, 2017), among others (for a broad discussion of such applications, see Jensen & Konradsen, 2018). Research exploring learning outcomes associated with AR/VR shows that students who use such technology experience affective activation through perceived presence and emotion, which, in turn, stimulates greater cognitive learning (Makransky & Lilleholt, 2018).

In 2017, Ohio University invested nearly $1M in the Immersive Media Initiative (IMI), a collaboration between the Scripps College of Communication and multiple partnering units intended to advance the university's capability in AR/VR training, development, and deployment. Since that investment, the IMI has developed niche expertise in medical education by using 360° video to create highly immersive training experiences for first responders, emergency room doctors and staff, and culturally based medical interview situations.

As the IMI expertise has developed, their ability to produce AR/VR content has accelerated in both quality and speed. In fall of 2018, the IMI team started developing AR/VR applications that could be widely used by anyone with a cell phone. For instance, we developed an AR poster that looks like a regular poster that would hang in any classroom. However, when viewed through a smartphone application, the poster comes alive with video, animations, and other multimedia. In other words, our poster application allows a traditional object to become completely interactive using AR/VR technology. We have also explored how AR/VR content can best be formatted for use by users with Google Cardboard or similar headsets. Our end objective is to build AR/VR educational content for different user levels, thus providing teachers and students with options for accessing content that are inexpensive. Although our content for premium headsets has already found strong adoption, particularly in the medical education space, we anticipate rapid growth by K-12 and college educators for content aimed at lower price-point options. We have already tested this concept in nine different K-12 classrooms in Ohio and received positive feedback from teachers.

How does AR/VR relate to our claim about the importance of ubiquitous technology in the classroom? Initial adoption of AR/VR technology was platform dependent. That is, most AR/VR content was intended for use by individuals with moderately expensive headsets. Now, AR/VR technology is crossing platforms to make greater use of common mobile technology. As content producers, like the IMI team, rapidly create immersive educational content, teachers will have vibrant options for teaching and learning in immersive environments. Our AR poster experiment is a harbinger for what will be commonplace in most classrooms without the need for new equipment— students' smartphones will be the primary platform through which they access the content.

Summary and Conclusion

Based on our own research showing that smart device use diminishes learning, one might suspect that we would strongly urge teachers to ban cell phone in class or at the very least strongly condemn such use. In fact, we are skeptical of such approaches. They are seemingly easy solutions that can actually cause more harm than good.

Returning to Verschelden (2017) argument in *Bandwidth Recovery*, we take at face value the proposition that when students are oppressed because of their race, economic status, gender preference, or other lived experiences, their bandwidth for learning is diminished. Though obviously not at the same level as discrimination, we feel that a similar effect may occur in some classrooms when teachers eschew smart devices. Students are psychologically (and perhaps physically

46 *Technology in the Classroom*

through wearable technologies like smart watches) intertwined with their devices. In fact, Gardiner (2016) argued that students are psychologically addicted to their phones. Thus, using course policies or other approaches to try and keep smart devices out of sight may actually create psychological barriers to learning.

Through our three examples—#turnitgold, ALCs, and AR/VR—we intended to show that smartphones and other ubiquitous technologies are potentially valuable learning tools in the classroom. In each case, students use their phones to expand their learning opportunities, collaborate with others, create products, and engage content. Those examples, for us, illustrate how use of smart devices can be potentially transitioned from problematic to productive because such use is intentionally integrated into learning.

We are realistic, but optimistic. Students who experienced #turnitgold, the ALC classroom, or who used AR/VR content very likely also perused social media, snapped a friend, and posted pictures to Instagram. Effective use of technology by the teacher cannot easily change habitual behaviors. At the same time, however, we believe that uses of ubiquitous technology improved learning experiences for students and helped them understand that their phones and other devices are important and useful tools for learning. In essence, smartphones are no different than any other disruptive teaching/communication technology. The rise of books meant that students did not have to obtain information solely through dialogue and lecture—the sophists were likely skeptical of books just as some of us are skeptical of mobile devices. However, finding ways to effectively integrate mobile technology into learning is an important step in reaching students where they are at. Like Verschelden (2017), we believe that such connection (i.e., meeting students where they are at) creates very powerful opportunities for learning.

References

Berry, M. J., & Westfall, A. (2015). Dial D for distraction: The making and breaking of cell phone policies in the college classroom. *College Teaching, 63*, 62–71. doi: 10.1080/87567555.2015.1005040

Bolkan, S., & Griffin, D. J. (2017). Students' use of cell phones in class for off-task behaviors: The indirect impact of instructors' teaching behaviors through boredom and students' attitudes. *Communication Education, 66*, 313–329. doi:10.1080/03634523.2016.1241888

Chandrasekera, T., & Yoon, S. Y. (2018). Augmented reality, virtual reality and their effect on learning style in the creative design process. *Design and Technology Education, 23*, 55–75.

The Active Classroom   47

Duncan, D. K., Hoekstra, A. R., & Wilcox, B. R. (2012). Digital devices, distraction, and student performance: Does in-class cell phone use reduce learning? *Astronomy Education Review, 11*. doi:10.3847/AER2012011

Entezari, M., & Javdan, M. (2016). Active learning and flipped classroom, hand in hand approach to improve students learning in human anatomy and physiology. *International Journal of Higher Education, 5*(4), 222–231. doi:10.5430/ijhe.v5n4p222

Federal Communication Commission. (2015, November 20). Jamming cell phones and GPS equipment is against the law. Bureau of Consumer and Governmental Affairs. Retrieved from https://www.fcc.gov/general/jamming-cell-phones-and-gps-equipment-against-law

Gardiner, S. (2016, 26 April). The student cell phone addiction is no joke. Education week [online]. Retrieved from http://www.edweek.org/ew/articles/2016/04/27/the-student-cellphone-addiction-is-no-joke.html

Gordy, X. Z., Jones, E. M., & Bailey, J. H. (2018). Technological innovation or educational evolution? A multidisciplinary qualitative inquiry into active learning classrooms. *Journal of the Scholarship of Teaching and Learning, 18*, 1–23. doi:10.14434/josotl.v18i2.23597

Hyun, J., Ediger, R., & Lee, D. (2017). Students' satisfaction on their learning process in active learning and traditional classrooms. *International Journal of Teaching and Learning in Higher Education, 29*, 108–118.

Jensen, L., & Konradsen, F. (2018). A review of the use of virtual reality head-mounted displays in education and training. *Education and Information Technologies, 23*(4), 1515–1529. doi:10.1007/s10639-017-9676-0

Johnson, L., Adams Becker, S., Cummins, M., Estrada, V., Freeman, A., & Hall, C. (2016). *NMC horizon report: 2016 higher education edition.* Austin, TX: The New Media Consortium.

Lancaster, A. L. (2018). Student learning with permissive and restrictive cell phone policies: A classroom experiment. *International Journal for the Scholarship of Teaching and Learning, 12*, 1–5. doi:10.20429/ijsotl.2018.120105

Makransky, G., & Lilleholt, L. (2018). A structural equation modeling investigation of the emotional value of immersive virtual reality in education. *Educational Technology Research and Development, 66*(5), 1141–1164. doi:10.1007/s11423-018-9581-2

Matyszczyk, C. (2015, June 3). Science teacher suspended for using jammer to shut up students' cell phones. *CNET* [Online]. Retrieved from https://www.cnet.com/news/science-teacher-suspended-for-using-jammer-to-shut-up-students-cell-phones/

Moro, C., Štromberga, Z., Raikos, A., & Stirling, A. (2017). The effectiveness of virtual and augmented reality in health sciences and medical anatomy. *Anatomical Sciences Education, 10*, 549–559. doi: 10.1002/ase.1696

Nicol, A. A. M., Owens, S. M., Le Coze, S. S. C. L., MacIntyre, A., & Eastwood, C. (2018). Comparison of high-technology active learning and low-technology active learning classrooms. *Active Learning in Higher Education, 19*(3), 253–265. doi:10.1177/1469787417731176

48 Technology in the Classroom

Orman, E. K., Price, H. E., & Russell, C. R. (2017). Feasibility of using an augmented immersive virtual reality learning environment to enhance music conducting skills. *Journal of Music Teacher Education, 27*, 24–35. doi:10.1177/1057083717697962

Sweeney, S. K., Newbill, P., Ogle, T., & Terry, K. (2018). Using augmented reality and virtual environments in historic places to scaffold historical empathy. *TechTrends: Linking Research and Practice to Improve Learning, 62*, 114–118. doi:10.1007/s11528-017-0234-9

Verschelden, C. (2017). *Bandwidth recovery: Helping students reclaim cognitive resources lost to poverty, racism, and social marginalization.* Sterling, VA: Stylus Publishing.

6 From Hardcopy to e-Book and e-Textbook Platforms

Introduction

Beginning with a narrative detailing the shift from hardcopy to digital book resources in the university classroom, this chapter examines the challenges posed by e-Book and e-Textbooks for student learning. While reading has remained a constant in higher education, the means through which the print word is presented and accessed has changed greatly. Advancements with technology have shifted from a static reading experience to one that is dynamic with re-flowable text, preference-based font type, size, page width, as well as educational components such as zoom resources for unfamiliar words and interactive questions to assist in making content connections. The digital immersive educational experiences provided by e-Books and e-Textbooks is predicated on students having the required skills to effectively access and utilize the technology. Through elucidating the complex relationship among digital resources and students' technological skills, we have much to learn about students' reading comprehension, higher-order knowledge gains, and adaptive assessment practices when it comes to e-Books and e-Textbooks.

As we move further into the digital age, our information-oriented society continues to enrich and saturate all aspects of our lived experiences. In this way, it is reasonable that the university student experience is also laden with the expectations of accessing e-Books and e-Textbooks (among other e-resources). Many educators may even believe that today's student embraces, understands, and is able to successfully utilize technology without educational consequences. While digital books are frequently favored for their cost-effectiveness and extensive supplementary resources, questions remain regarding their educational benefits for both digital native (or those born after the rise of technology) and digital immigrant students (or those prior to the rise of technology), with both concepts being discussed in depth in Chapter 3.

50 *Technology in the Classroom*

The focus of this chapter will be examining the issues surrounding e-Books and e-Textbooks in the university classroom. First, a short history detailing the infusion of e-Books and e-Textbooks into the university classroom will be distilled. Next, students learning experiences related to digital reading from recent scholarly research are examined. Finally, a discussion regarding the nuances of digital versus print reading is presented.

From Old to *New* Book

The book has and continues (for the time being at least) to be the foundation of a students' educational experience. And while reading continues to be a constant for a students' learning experience, the experience s/he may incur with a text has changed greatly. Sometime half-way through the first-decade of the twenty-first century, the first e-Books were released into the digital marketplace (Merkoski, 2013). In the beginning, e-Books were classics, popular press books, and a litany of other genres such as self-help, motivational/inspirational, and hobbyist books. Although, Amazon and its e-reader Kindle have become synonymous with e-Books and digital reading, Merkoski (2013) argues that it was in fact thinkers at Sony in 2003 who presented an e-reader into the Japanese marketplace. In 2006, Sony executives brought their Sony e-reader into the U.S. marketplace, and in 2007, Amazon launched the first generation of the Kindle. The invention of the Kindle by Amazon, many argue, revolutionized the process to find, buy and download, and access e-Books. And with each subsequent generation of the Kindle, Amazon has only increased the sophistication and expectations for the e-reading experience.

Although e-Books are well established for reading outside of the educational setting, only recently e-Textbooks have gained greater focus and priority. Many argue that because e-Books caused a disruption in the hardcopy book marketplace, textbook publishers began to transform their content digitally to meet the demands of consumers and match the changes in the publishing industry. However as Weisberg (2011) argues higher education is characterized as a "dynamic tension between tradition and innovation" (p. 196). Eventually, textbook publishers were also faced with the reality of increasing numbers of technologically savvy students and instructors who were also demanding the integration of technology into the educational environment. Once hardcopy textbook content was transferred to static e-Books, the next step included embedding innovative digital features such as searchable text, interactive tables and figures, links to videos

From Hardcopy to e-Book and e-Textbook Platforms 51

and sound clips, and the capability for students to add digital notes. The added features embedded into e-Textbooks facilitate an interactive and engaging reading platform, therefore, changing the student reading experience. No longer are there simply words on a page, for today's student reading is laden with multimedia and interactivity, but are such changes helpful for student learning?

Student Learning

Today, many students embrace and embed technology into their lives in ways that previous generations may strain to even imagine possible. Although e-Textbooks are increasingly becoming more cost-effective (see Johnson, 2016), convenient to access and portable (see Hernon, Hopper, Leach, Saunders, & Zhang, 2007; Kiriakova, Okamoto, Zubarev, & Gross, 2010) when compared to hardcopy books, there are still unanswered questions about students' learning experiences. It is important to establish that the research regarding the influences of e-Books or e-Textbooks on student learning is in its infancy. However, the existing research does illuminate some interesting findings, which we believe inspire further questions about digital books and student learning. Sun, Flores, and Tanguma (2012) examined e-Textbook and student learning experiences and established that e-Textbooks effect students differently depending on their level of involvement. In their study, students who believed the e-Textbook (and added features) were helpful also believed that it would enhance learning outcomes. However, students who did not believe that the e-Textbook was helpful did not use it for classroom experiences and learning. In short, the takeaway for instructors is that simple exposure to an e-Textbook does not equate to student learning or increased involvement in class. Rather students must view the e-Textbook as merit worthy for their learning and have directed engagement with the book from their instructor.

It is widely accepted that effective instruction in the classroom can positively influence students' learning experiences. In examining student learning and e-Textbooks, O'Bannon, Skolits, and Lubke (2017) forward that students who received lecture instruction in the classroom as well as instruction through a digital book platform outperformed students who only received lecture instruction from the instructor. While this finding is intriguing, it matches our expectations that students who receive additional instruction would outperform students who do not. From these results, questions emerge regarding how students engage with interactive instruction as well as how their attitude or motivation toward electronics contributes

52 *Technology in the Classroom*

to their learning experience. Further, O'Bannon et al. (2017) assert that one of the additional benefits of using digital books is that it "made learning more exciting, [and] increased their attention toward instruction" (O'Bannon et al., 2017, p. 112). Investigating the differences between students who have an affinity and readiness for tablets and e-readers for learning in the classroom may provide useful results.

Further elucidating additional concerns with e-Textbooks, Weisberg (2011) posits that it is valuable to understand students' prior experiences with digital devices because "they do not currently see their laptop or computer as a replacement for a textbook" (p. 192). Students may very well value the ease and flexibility of being able to access their textbook digitally, however fail to make the connection that while on their laptop reading they are in fact supposed to be engaging in deep learning (Weisberg, 2011). This finding suggests that while students may have favorable experiences with e-Textbooks, the medium they engage their book on is an important factor. Thereby suggesting that there are possibly differences between accessing an e-Textbook on an electronic tablet versus an e-reader device. Relatedly, Daniel and Woody (2013) explain one noteworthy concern for educators includes not if, but how much, multitasking students are doing while reading their e-Textbook. That is, if students are on their laptops, cell phones, or tablets, they more easily can access the web and social media sites in comparison to if they are using e-readers with no web browsing capabilities. Given the research on the negative effects of multitasking on student learning (see Chapter 2), the implementation of e-Textbooks via web accessible electronic mediums is concerning as they may influence students study habits and consequently learning.

Implementing e-Textbooks in the university classroom, like any technological resource, requires consideration for the influence on students' educational experiences. Often students, and educators alike, rush to acquire a "new" technology and falsely assume it will be superior to the "old." In the classroom, such decisions can either increase or decrease students' motivation, which can cause difficulties for student learning (Hortsch, 2015). Through considering the importance of internal and external motivation as they relate to student learning and e-Textbooks, Johnson (2016 concludes that the differences among student book purchases (e-Textbook or paper-text) was predicted by intrinsic (e.g., challenging learning content) or extrinsic motivation (e.g., grades or peer approval). Students who were motivated by external factors were more likely to purchase paper textbooks, while

From Hardcopy to e-Book and e-Textbook Platforms 53

students motivated by internal factors were more likely to purchase e-Textbooks (Johnson, 2016). This finding is intriguing, considering young people are typically more likely to adopt and utilize technology; however, in the context of learning students may be reluctant to fully adopt innovations such as e-Textbooks.

We must also consider whether or not students have the necessary skills, experiences, and knowledge dexterity to successfully utilize an e-Textbook. An e-Textbook and accompanying digital resources are novel educational experiences, however may come at consequence if students (1) prefer traditional print texts or (2) are apprehensive about utilizing the e-Textbook/digital platform. Addressing students preferences with e-Textbooks or print texts, Johnson (2016) posits that only students who self-described themselves as competent learners preferred e-Textbooks. While self-perception does not necessary reflect reality, such a finding does illuminate the necessity for further exploration into this topic.

Digital versus Print Reading

At the heart of the argument on whether or not to integrate e-Books and e-Textbooks into the university classroom is the question regarding if students will *deeply* read the material. There is no question that electronic texts are lighter and more convenient for students to grab—especially on the go. However, research suggests to exercise caution when assuming students' levels of comprehension with printed and e-Book materials are similar. Through their study, Ackerman and Goldsmith (2011) posit that students performed better on comprehension questions when reading in print in comparison to digitally. It is difficult to know whether such a finding is a result of visual eye fatigue, refresh rate, or contrast levels on the screen (Ackerman & Goldsmith, 2011). While Ackerman and Goldsmith (2011) assessed students' reading comprehension through short answer questions, Connell, Bayliss, and Framer (2012), who assessed students' reading comprehension through a 40-item pre post-test design, found no difference in students' reading comprehension scores. Such conflicting results are prevalent throughout the literature and can be attributed to differences in assessment and merit future systematic examination. In short, there are lingering questions about the differences between digital and print reading as it relates to students' reading comprehension.

Students and educators alike hold positive and negative views in regard to digital reading. However, students who self-identify as

54 Technology in the Classroom

digital natives (see Chapter 3 for more in-depth discussion) often prefer and classify digital reading as easier and more accessible (Singer & Alexander, 2017a). In their study, Connell et al. (2012) reveal that students' reading comprehension was unaffected by the text formats of hardcopy paper, Kindle, or iPad with a backlit display. However, the medium the text was presented on did significantly influence reading time, with hardcopy text being the most efficient in regard to reading time (Connell et al., 2012). While the reading comprehension scores are positive, we find the increased time students spent reading the text electronically worrisome for student learning. If students are spending longer reading a text electronically, there are questions about how longer or more challenging texts may influence student learning. Finally, we must also consider the implications for deep reading or internalization, memorization, as well as information recall when discussing the differences between paper and electronic reading.

Explorations into the differences between students' reading comprehension through an e-Textbook or a paper book are at best inconclusive and worthy of further investigation. In part, this is a result of the relative newness of e-Textbooks and other electronic resources from publishers (Rockinson-Szapkiw, Courduff, Carter, & Bennett, 2013), however can also be attributed to the challenges of assessing cognitive learning. According to Rockinson-Szapkiw et al. (2013), students who utilized an e-Textbook as compared to a print textbook had equivalent or better attitudes toward subject matter content. Students who utilized an e-Textbook also perceived higher skills acquisition too. Taken together, if reading course content via an e-Textbook potentially improves students' attitudes about learning and skills, then it is reasonable to assert the possibility of positive improvements to students' attitudes and motivation to read. While these findings are promising, they fail to address, how if at all, reading comprehension would be influenced. Examining how students' self-study regulation of their reading on electronic versus print texts would influence learning performances, Ackerman and Goldsmith (2011) found that students who studied on paper outperformed students who read electronically by 10%. Such results reveal important differences in metacognition between the two mediums, which may suggest variances in the learning processes and potentially the skills required for learning via electronic and print texts.

Finally, descriptively speaking, reading an e-Textbook in comparison to a print book presents different experiences for the reader.

Baron (2015) argues that "computers and now tablets and mobile phones were not designed for lengthy, focused reading" (p. 211). Even more so, in our minds, the connotation of reading as it is associated with digital platforms versus traditional print is likely also differentiated. This differentiation informs how we approach and influences our engagement with the medium. One possible explanation for the differences in students' reading comprehension is noted as the "disruptive effect" or the influence of scrolling (Singer & Alexander, 2017a). When considering students' recall after reading a text, Singer and Alexander (2017b) found that students recalled key points as they related to the main idea of a text better when they read in print versus digitally. Such a finding is interesting, when considering the fact that students indicated a preference for reading electronically and even predicated better comprehension outcomes when reading digitally (Singer & Alexander, 2017b). While a student's preference is important, it must also be considered with caution because it may arise from an over confidence in abilities. Additional research is needed to examine the specific reasons for students' preferences between print and e-Textbooks.

Concluding Thoughts

There are many complexities that come with implementing e-Textbooks or e-Books in a university classroom. Lingering questions about the differences in student learning resulting from print versus e-Textbooks remain unanswered and merit further investigation. While some scholarship suggests similar learning experiences for students utilizing print and e-Textbooks, there remain unanswered questions about the differences in learning experiences. Innovative educators might be more likely to implement e-Textbooks in their classrooms, while later adopters of technology will wait for a clearer answer to the influence of this tool on student learning. All educators should carefully consider integrating technology in the classroom, and we suggest viewing an e-Textbook similarly. That is, while there are potential benefits, there are also a number of issues such as note-taking, reading short-cuts (or scanning), eye fatigue, content length and reading time worthy of consideration before adopting an e-Textbook. Further, we are faced with questions of whether or not students should be afforded choice in the platform of their book and whether or not publishers can cost-effectively bundle both a print and e-Textbook to students. In short, there are no simple answers on whether it is best for students to read in print or digitally.

56 Technology in the Classroom

The ubiquity of technology within the digital age will continue to permeate our classrooms and as educators, we are faced with the implications of digital innovation on student learning.

References

Ackerman, R., & Goldsmith, M. (2011). Metacognitive regulation of text learning: On screen versus on paper. *Journal of Experimental Psychology. Applied, 17*(1), 18–32. doi:10.1037/a0022086

Baron, N. S. (2015). *Words onscreen: The fate of reading in a digital world.* New York, NY: Oxford University Press.

Connell, C., Bayliss, L., & Farmer, W. (2012). Effects of eBook readers and tablet computers on reading comprehension. *International Journal of Instructional Media, 39*(2), 131–140.

Daniel, D. B., & Woody, W. D. (2013). E-textbooks at what cost? Performance and use of electronic v. print texts. *Computers & Education, 62,* 18–23. doi:10.1016/j.compedu.2012.10.016

Hernon, P., Hopper, R., Leach, M. R., Saunders, L. L., & Zhang, J. (2007). E-book use by students: Undergraduates in economics, literature, and nursing. *The Journal of Academic Librarianship, 33*(1), 3–13. doi:10.1016/j. acalib.2006.08.005

Hortsch, M. (2015). 'How we learn may not always be good for us'—Do new electronic teaching approaches always result in better learning outcomes? *Medical Teacher, 37*(6), 507–509. doi:10.3109/0142159X.2014.1001341

Johnson, G. M. (2016). The influence of student learning characteristics on purchase of paper book and eBook for university study and personal interest. *Educational Psychology, 36*(9), 1544–1559. doi:10.1080/01443410.2014.1002831

Kiriakova, M., Okamoto, K. S., Zubarev, M., & Gross, G. (2010). Aiming at a moving target: Pilot testing eBook readers in an urban academic library. *Computers in Libraries, 30*(2), 20–24.

Merkoski, J. (2013). *Burning the page: The eBook revolution and the future of reading.* Naperville, IL: Sourcebooks.

O'Bannon, B. W., Skolits, G. J., & Lubke, J. K. (2017). The influence of digital interactive textbook instruction on student learning preferences, outcomes, and motivation. *Journal of Research on Technology in Education, 49*(3/4), 103–116. doi:10.1080/15391523.2017.1303798

Rockinson-Szapkiw, A. J., Courduff, J., Carter, K., & Bennett, D. (2013). Electronic versus traditional print textbooks: A comparison study on the influence of university students' learning. *Computers & Education, 63,* 259–266. doi:10.1016/j.compedu.2012.11.022

Singer, L. M., & Alexander, P. A. (2017a). Reading across mediums: Effects of reading digital and print texts on comprehension and calibration. *The Journal of Experimental Education, 85*(1), 155–172. doi:10.1080/00220973.2016.1143794

From Hardcopy to e-Book and e-Textbook Platforms 57

Singer, L. M., & Alexander, P. A. (2017b). Reading on paper and digitally: What the past decades of empirical research reveal. *Review of Educational Research, 87*(6), 1007–1041. doi:10.3102/0034654317722961

Sun, J., Flores, J., & Tanguma, J. (2012). E-textbooks and students' learning experiences. *Decision Sciences Journal of Innovative Education, 10*(1), 63–77. doi:10.1111/j.1540-4609.2011.00329.x

Weisberg, M. (2011). Student attitudes and behaviors towards digital textbooks. *Publishing Research Quarterly, 27*(2), 188–196. doi:10.1007/s12109-011-9217-4

7 Online Learning

Introduction

No conversation of technology and learning would be complete without including a discussion concerning the online classroom. Indeed, entire books have been written to go in depth on issues including instructional technology (Anglin, 2011), course design (Vai & Sosulski, 2015), online teaching (McCabe & González-Flores, 2016), and accessibility for students with disabilities (Coombs, 2010). By no means, this is an all-encompassing list, but these examples help to illustrate the broad range of issues that come up in any discussion of the online classroom. Most certainly, this is an important and emerging area of higher education, these discussions will continue as technology develops further and as higher education adapts to those changes. Thus, the goal of this chapter is to discuss online learning but, more importantly, to offer a different perspective by focusing on the critiques of the online classroom and concerns that many faculty have in this area.

Growth of Online

The growth of online degree programs and classes is one of the top issues in higher education since the turn of the century. According to the National Center for Education Statistics (2018), in fall 2015, nearly 6 million college students were enrolled in distance education courses in the United States, and out of the nearly 20 million college students at the time, roughly 14% were enrolled in programs that were exclusively distance education. In the United States, the number of online students has grown considerably, from under 2.5 million in fall 2002 to roughly 7 million in fall 2011. Furthermore, during this rough timespan, the proportion of college students taking at least one online course increased from less than 10% in fall 2003 to likely over 30% (Allen & Seaman, 2013). This trend is unlikely to change, and we expect that online classes and degree programs to continue to expand in the coming years.

Without a doubt, online learning has become a substantial part of higher education and nearly every college or university in the U.S. is likely grappling with how best to approach online learning. Certainly, some schools are jumping head first into online learning and fully investing into online education. Indeed, you have likely viewed commercials either on television or through an online advertisement that feature either an online degree program or a university that caters specifically to online students. Most brick and mortar schools have also developed, to one degree or another, online course offerings and/or online degree programs. However, we argue that an important consideration is a balanced approach to the discussion concerning online learning. From our experiences, the discussions in this realm are often focused almost exclusively on the advantages of online classes, particularly that students can complete assignments at their own pace or on their own schedule, and that fully online classes do not require students to be physically present in a classroom. However, the downsides, which can be considerable, are often overlooked or discussed in passing. In our experience, it is often rather easy for students to ignore course-related messages and miss out on important content or to be digitally absent from the online classroom (i.e., still enrolled in the class but not turning in assignments or participating). As faculty who have developed and taught online classes, expanding this conversation to include negative aspects of online learning is certainly needed.

Deconstructing Online Learning

Overall, faculty are relatively divided about whether online courses achieve similar outcomes as traditional classes, while those in charge of online learning are more convinced of online classes reaching higher-order learning outcomes (Jaschik & Lederman, 2013, 2017). In addition, faculty have consistently remained cautious about online education. For example, Allen, Seaman, Lederman, and Jaschik (2012) report:

> Professors, over all, cast a skeptical eye on the learning outcomes for online education. Nearly two-thirds say they believe that the learning outcomes for an online course are inferior or somewhat inferior to those for a comparable face-to-face course. Most of

60　*Technology in the Classroom*

the remaining faculty members report that the two have comparable outcomes. Even among those with a strong vested interest in online education – faculty members who are currently teaching online courses – considerable concern remains about the quality of the learning outcomes.

(p. 2)

This sentiment still appears to be the case; however, attitudes may slowly be changing. For instance, in 2013, only 7% of surveyed faculty members strongly agreed that online courses could achieve equivalent student learning outcomes as face-to-face (FtF) courses, while 27% of educational technology administrators strongly agreed with that statement. Four years later, those figures were 11% for faculty and 55% for digital learning leaders (Jaschik & Lederman, 2017).

Even though perceptions may be changing, we do see evidence that faculty are generally skeptical of the effectiveness of online learning. Meanwhile, online learning leaders or people on the administrative side of higher education appear to be very supportive of online learning in general. For example, 50% of college presidents expected that, in a decade, most of their students would be taking online classes (Parker, Lenhart, & Moore, 2011). However, recent reports seem to indicate that online classes and degree programs may indeed cost students and institutions more. Newton (2018) summarized several research reports and notes that "It can cost more than $1,000 to find and enroll a single online student" (¶. 10) and that "most colleges charge the same or more for their online programs as they do for their traditional, in-person offerings" (¶. 1). This diversion in attitudes, as well as potential additional costs to students and institutions, is an important consideration. Faculty, the people who are directly in contact with students in their traditional or virtual classroom, appear to be fairly hesitant with how effective online learning truly is. This should be a point of caution as higher education adapts to online learning and as we question what place online learning should have in a college degree. In addition, we should also consider the important learning interactions that are reduced or removed as we move from FtF to online classes.

What Is Lost in the Online Classroom?

Beyond the debate concerning online versus traditional classes, an important consideration is what is lost in online classes. For instance, students lose direct, FtF contact with instructors and important experience interacting in an FtF environment. For example, students who rely too heavily on due date reminders from their institution's learning management system (LMS) may not develop important planning skills, and although online classes do have collaborative spaces like text-based discussion boards, the efficacy of those spaces remains questionable at best.

Davies and Graff (2005) examined Blackboard discussions in online classes, one of the primary student-to-student modes of interaction in the online classroom. Their study found that "students who interacted and participated more in online discussions in this study did not necessarily achieve higher grades" (Davies & Graff, 2005, p. 662). Furthermore, Davies and Graff link in additional research (Weisskirch & Milburn, 2003) to offer that voluntary online course interaction may be more beneficial to student learning than instructor required online interactions. By no means is this research conclusive, and certainly, the online classroom and LMSs have changed quite a bit in the past decade; however, modern text-based discussion boards still share the base-level structure and functionality with their decade-old versions.

Assessing student learning at the lesson, course, and program level is of great importance at all levels of a student's academic life. Indeed, online faculty and course designers are likely familiar with programs or organizations that provide guidance or rubrics to assess the quality of an online course. However, faculty may question if these widely used online assessment practices are effective in helping faculty understand student learning. Stallard and Cocker (2015) discuss LMS applications and that assessment practices should help educators to understand the needs of individual students. However, it appears as though the typical assessment practices used in online classes "do not provide levels of insight into individual readiness and day-to-day progress that is needed" (Stallard & Cocker, 2015, p. 15). Furthermore, the typical form these assessment practices take is some sort of quiz or other basic assessment at the end of a particular learning unit or module. Stallard and Cocker note:

> too often these are oversimplified checks for understanding at a given moment when what is needed is a comprehensive understanding of the learner's acquired ability in a discipline or skill and readiness for the next level of complexity within that discipline.
>
> (2015, p. 15)

62 Technology in the Classroom

We would argue that the online learning environment may make it difficult to assess student acquired ability, certainly when juxtaposed against the traditional FtF classroom. In a physical class, instructors can monitor a host of student behaviors and nonverbal messages that are often filtered out in the online classroom. Certainly, assessment of student learning can and does happen in the online environment, but many instructors may find this more difficult and may take longer than in a traditional classroom.

Gonzales, Calarco, and Lynch (2018) note that college students nearly universally own mobile phones and laptops; however, maintaining consistent access to this technology, particularly if a device breaks, can represent a particular hardship for students. This hardship is especially the case for students who come from a lower socioeconomic status (SES). For example, Gonzales et al. (2018) note that "half of students (51%) had at some point been unable to complete coursework due to problems with technology, and 36% had asked for an extension due to technology problems" (p. 11). This becomes even more problematic when we consider that a primary means through which instructors communicate with students outside the classroom is through email and/or LMS announcements or messages. Understandably, students who lose access to their devices may also miss out an important course-related content or messages, and this is further problematized when the method of instruction is fully online. In addition, "students who had more poorly functioning laptops and laptops that broke down more often also had lower GPAs, even after accounting for SES and other demographic covariates" (Gonzales et al., 2018, p. 11). Lastly, the authors note that nearly half of the students in their study would need at least two weeks to replace a laptop or mobile phone if it failed. The added requirement of access to not only a computer but also stable internet connection is certainly an obvious need in an online classroom, and faculty may very well assume that students have ready access to both through campus resources. However, this view doesn't take into consideration distance students or those online students who may never physically visit campus. These students, and students who would financially struggle to replace technology needed to access course content, are left to fend for themselves. Although technology might also be needed in an FtF classroom, we would expect that students would be able to at least partially participate in a class, something that might not be possible in an online class in which a student loses complete access.

Different Views of Online Programs

Another area of online learning needing consideration is how different perspectives view online learning. In general, it would appear that many who have taken an online class tend to report favorable views of their online education. Parker et al. (2011) report that 39% of adults who have taken an online class report that the educational value of online classes was equal to that of traditional, FtF classes. However, only 29% of the general public agreed with that sentiment, and 51% of college presidents held that view. Put another way:

> Adults who have taken a course online have a somewhat more positive view of the value of this learning format: 39% say a course taken online provides the same educational value as one taken in person, a view shared by only 27% of those who have not taken an online course.
>
> (Parker et al., 2011, p. 3)

Research examining the perceptions of human resource managers notes that nearly half of their respondents believed their organization did not view online degree graduates as being equivalent to traditional degree graduates (Kaupins, Wanek, & Coco, 2014).

Often overlooked in the discussion of developing online classes or degree programs is the perception that others, outside of academia, have about online degree programs. At least some of the evidence seems to indicate that a large portion of either human resource managers or the general public do not equate online degrees as equivalent to FtF degrees. This is an important consideration and one that will likely develop over time. However, at present, it appears that there is still a stigma associated with online education, and this is an important point to make as departments and academic divisions contemplate their online strategies. In addition, students should carefully consider this point as they pursue online degrees.

Summary

Without question, online learning is here to stay and online classes do serve an important purpose. Online classes and degree programs can reach populations that have typically had limited access to higher education and we should continue to reach out to these students. However, researchers have pointed out that many faculty are

64 *Technology in the Classroom*

resistant to the move to more online classes, and public opinion polling seems to note that a large portion of the public do not equate online classes as equivalent to FtF classes. Online learning certainly has a place in higher education; however, we should be cautious with moving to develop more classes and degree programs. Online education is not a panacea for the significant issues facing higher education institutions but likely is one of many potential solutions to those problems.

References

Allen, I. E., & Seaman, J. (2013). *Changing course: Ten years of tracking online education in the United States.* Retrieved from http://www.onlinelearningsurvey.com/reports/changingcourse.pdf

Allen, I. E., Seaman, J., Lederman, D., & Jaschik, S. (2012). *Conflicted: Faculty and online education, 2012.* Retrieved from https://files.eric.ed.gov/fulltext/ED535214.pdf

Anglin, G. J. (Ed.). (2011). *Instructional technology: Past, present, and future* (3rd ed.). Santa Barbara, CA: ABD-CLIO.

Coombs, N. (2010). *Making online teaching accessible: Inclusive course design for students with disabilities.* San Francisco, CA: Jossey-Bass.

Davies, J., & Graff, M. (2005). Performance in e-learning: Online participation and student grades. *British Journal of Educational Technology, 36,* 657–663.

Gonzales, A. L., Calarco, J. M., & Lynch, T. (2018). Technology problems and student achievement gaps: A validation and extension of the technology maintenance construct. *Communication Research.* doi:10.1177/0093650218796366

Jaschik, S., & Lederman, D. (2013). *The 2013 inside higher ed survey of faculty attitudes on technology: Conducted by Gallup.* Retrieved from https://www.insidehighered.com/system/files/media/IHE_FacultySurvey-final.pdf

Jaschik, S., & Lederman, D. (2017). *2017 survey of faculty attitudes on technology: A study by inside higher ed and gallup.* Retrieved from https://www.insidehighered.com/booklet/2017-survey-faculty-attitudes-technology

Kaupins, G. E., Wanek, J. E., & Coco, M. P. (2014). The relationship of HR professionals online experiences with perceptions of organizational hiring and promotion of online graduates. *Journal of Education for Business, 89,* 222–229. doi:10.1080/08832323.2013.852076

McCabe, M. F., & González-Flores, P. (2016). *Essentials of online teaching: A standards-based guide* (1st ed.). New York, NY: Routledge, Taylor & Francis Group.

National Center for Education Statistics. (2018). *Digest of education statistics, 2016.* NCES 2017–094, Table 311.15.

Newton, D. (2018, June 25). Why college tuition is actually higher for online programs. Retrieved from https://www.forbes.com/sites/dereknewton/2018/06/25/why-college-tuition-is-actually-higher-for-online-programs/#18c94811f11a

Parker, K., Lenhart, A., & Moore, K. (2011). *The digital revolution and higher education: College presidents, public differ on value of online learning.* Retrieved from http://www.pewresearch.org/wp-content/uploads/sites/3/2011/08/online-learning.pdf

Stallard, C. K., & Cocker, J. (2015). *Education technology and the failure of American schools.* Lanham, MD: Rowman & Littlefield.

Weisskirch, R. S., & Milburn, S. S. (2003). Virtual discussion: Understanding college students' electronic bulletin board use. *The Internet and Higher Education, 6*(3), 215–225.

Vai, M., & Sosulski, K. (2015). *Essentials of online course design* (2nd ed.). New York, NY: Routledge, Taylor & Francis Group.

Part 4

Technology and Academic Audiences

8 Considerations for Teachers

Introduction

At its core, the profession of teaching still maintains a strong connection to the history of the professoriate dating back to Aristotle. However, the notion that technology in education is new is not entirely accurate. Since moving away from an oral society, technology has been involved in teaching and learning. As far back as chalk and writing slates, or the widespread use of chalk boards and white boards through educational levels, technology was a tool through which teachers can help convey knowledge to students. Certainly, that technology has grown in type and capability, but it still maintains the same function: to help teachers convey information to students to help them understand that information and learn from it. In this chapter, we caution against teachers jumping on the tech bandwagon. We argue that, by itself, technology will not improve learning in meaningful ways. Instead, technology paired with thoughtful pedagogy and teacher training may hold the key to meaningfully integrating technology into the classroom. Instructors must mindfully embrace changes to their teaching practices in the classroom, while also ensuring that such changes are built upon evidenced based research and with the best interests of students in mind.

This chapter counters the error of equating the use of technology in the classroom as increasing student learning and success. While effective pedagogy in the classroom remains a primary goal, teachers today must contend with changing technological mediums and platforms and their relationship with student learning. The use of mobile devices, laptops, and tablets are often positioned as providing educational benefits in the classroom. However, with little pedagogical training to purposefully integrate the use of such technological devices or substantial evidence-based research to support the claims

70   *Technology and Academic Audiences*

of increased student learning, instructors must mindfully embrace changes to their teaching practices in the classroom.

This chapter will engage the aforementioned concerns of implementing technology in the classroom, with careful attention to the influence, if any, on student learning. First, examined in this chapter is the complex landscape of technology in the classroom. Next, a conceptual framework for understanding the relationship between technology and pedagogy is presented. Finally, this chapter will conclude with a discussion of the importance of teacher preparation and technology.

Technology in Today's Classroom

As the world becomes increasingly more technologically driven, the classroom is also becoming a context permeated with the expectations of technological tools. Brick and mortar classrooms are now rife with clickers, laptops, tablets, engagement quizzes via mobile phones, and e-Textbooks embedded with adaptive reading prompts. Even the conceptualization of the classroom has shifted from face-to-face to online and hybrid experiences for students. Today, individuals are also able to participate in web-based learning through massive open online courses (MOOCs) or small open online courses (SMOOCs) which provides cost-free educational experiences. Hortsch (2015) asserts that in many ways technology has rendered "classrooms obsolete" (p. 507). While Hortsch's (2015) claim is an exaggerated assertion, many educators agree that a paradigmatic shift as a result of technology has occurred in the classroom. Students expect instructors to engage with technology proficiently and fully both through instruction and in the design of assignments.

Through examining the various technologies implemented in the classroom, we can appreciate the ways in which innovations have changed, improved, and even replaced other modes of instruction. The advent of Microsoft's PowerPoint and Apple's Keynote slideshow programs altered academic lecturers. Lectures now have the capacity to offer multiple modes of engagement through pictures, video, and audio clips; however, on the other hand, slideshow presentations are often feared by audiences who worry about being the victims of death by PowerPoint (Hedges, 2014). Slideshow programs, many argue, fundamentally shifted students' expectations for content delivered in the classroom. Today, students expect their instructor to deliver content multimodally, which is a significant shift away from the days of students passively absorbing knowledge (Okojie, 2011). Although the goal of a teacher to effectively deliver content in order for students to transfer and apply knowledge remains consistent, it is unclear whether technology always positively enhances student learning or the effectiveness of instructor delivery.

Through relational or rhetorical schemas, communication researchers have widely examined instructor pedagogy and communication messages in the classroom in pursuit of understanding students learning experiences and the influence of instructor messages (see Mottet & Beebe, 2006, for a discussion of instructor and student messages in the classroom). The relational perspective forwards that "both teachers and students mutually create and use verbal and nonverbal messages" to form relationships in the classroom (Mottet & Beebe, 2006, p. 24). While the rhetorical perspective examines how a teacher utilizes "verbal and nonverbal messages with the intention of influencing or persuading students" (Mottet & Beebe, 2006, p. 23). However, as Hosek and Titsworth (2016) argue, these traditional approaches fail to account for how technology permeates the ways in which millennial students access and learn in the classroom. For example, today, students access content in multiple forms (e.g., e-Books, vlogs, websites), and as a result of the changing technological landscape may have more agile learning preferences. Suggesting that more traditional forms of media such as PowerPoint presentations in the classroom may fail to enhance or even empower student learning.

The ways in which students engage with their instructor have also shifted as a result of technology. Often students opt to email with questions about course content, assignments, or upcoming course due dates rather than stopping by office hours. Students expect to be able to access and connect with their instructor in ways that match their personal learning preferences (Boruszko, 2013). In this way, students also anticipate utilizing technology to connect with their instructors well beyond class time. For example, with increasingly more elementary and secondary education schools implementing learning management systems (LMSs), students enter the university classroom with similar or even increased communication expectations for their university professors. Boruszko (2013) argues that today students engage with professors beyond class time "through forums in all kinds of media" (p. 2). Students expect to reach their instructor through an LMS with ease and efficiency and expect a timely response, too. Perhaps as a result of being immersed in a digital world, students today expect a similar responsiveness from an email to their instructor as they would receive from mobile texting.

72 *Technology and Academic Audiences*

Technology and Pedagogy

While there are a variety of conceptions and approaches to the use of technology in the classroom, there seem to be two ways to frame the relationship between technology and pedagogy. We can categorize the approaches into either (1) *teaching focused* or (2) *learning focused*. These categories are useful for understanding an instructor's motivation for implementing technology in the classroom. According to Kirkwood and Price (2013), a teaching-focused approach entails "teaching being considered to be primarily about the transmission of information, skills, and attitudes" (p. 328). A teaching-focused instructor is more likely to implement technology into their pedagogical practices because mediums such as a PowerPoint or Keynote would supplement their instructional practices. Whereas Kirkwood and Price (2013) detail a learning-focused approach as "promoting the development of conceptual understanding in students" (p. 328). A learning-focused instructor is more likely to integrate technology in the classroom to support student learning. Through considering technology in relation to these two approaches, we can better understand the motivation for some teachers implement technological tools, while other instructors may favor a technology-free classroom. Aligned with scholarly research, which often argues for students to have choice and voice in their learning experience, we argue that similar considerations should be given to teachers too—especially when considering technology.

For an instructor, there are numerous intricacies within a classroom that requires readiness and preparation. Highlighting the complexities of the classroom, scholars have emphasized the importance of instructors understanding both their own behaviors as well as students' nuanced learning experiences (see McCroskey, Richmond, & McCroskey, 2002; Mottet, Richmond, & McCroskey, 2006). While the scholarship of teaching and learning is rich in many regards, tensions remain regarding the relationship between technology and pedagogy. Addressing these concerns, Meloncon (2007) suggests understanding these tensions through situating the instructor at the center of the electronic landscape (e.g., personal, pedagogical, managerial, technical, and institutional concerns). In this way, instructors should be encouraged to purposefully consider how a digital technology tool is utilized in the classroom. When presented with the choice of implementing technological tools or textbook supplements in their classroom, Sellnow, Child, and Ahlfeldt (2005) forward that instructors chose to reduce the number of digital technology tools.

An instructor must determine whether or not s/he is comfortable coordinating the implementation of a technological tool for student learning.

As technology continues to pervade the classroom setting, instructors are expected to implement engagement strategies, experiential activities, and higher-order learning experiences for students. The pressures and competing demands placed on an instructor today make it seem as if the newness, speed, or efficiency of a technological device will create time-saving pedagogical rewards. However, such thinking is problematic because it endorses the notion of "technological determinism" or the conception that a technology will *"in and of itself"* improve teaching (Kirkwood & Price, 2013, p. 333). Such thinking fails to acknowledge the consequences of adopting technology such as social media sites, clickers, tablets, or mobile devices on student learning. An instructor must evaluate whether s/he chooses to implement a technological tool in the classroom, while remembering that the human element integral to pedagogy is never fully replaced. Rather technology should be viewed as an additive to instruction. When viewed as complimenting or in harmony with classroom instruction, the teacher remains the agent, creator, or designer of educational activities in the promotion of learning in the classroom (Kirkwood & Price, 2013). In this way, the instructor implements technology in order to enable desired learning outcomes.

Teacher Preparation and Technology

In order for a teacher to utilize technology in the classroom, s/he often requires professional development in order to effectively integrate technology for student learning. While teacher preparation training has largely focused on instructional skills (e.g., clarity, immediacy, discussion facilitation and classroom management techniques, among other topics), it seems an assumption remains that instructors are already prepared to effectively implement technology in the classroom. Within a learning context, the assumption is that teachers have the knowledge and training to integrate, utilize, and engage students through technology. Perhaps as a result of already being a user of technology (e.g., laptop, tablet, or internet) or as result of being younger, a conception exists that an instructor can make sense and successfully implement a tech-tool. However, effective teaching requires forethought and a strategy for transmitting information to students in order for learning to occur.

74 *Technology and Academic Audiences*

Without training or preparation to implement a digital tool, instructors risk negatively influencing their credibility as well as student learning.

When considering digital tools in the classroom, teacher preparation must instill a philosophy of being a lifelong learner. That is, a teacher's conception of what it means to be an educator and learner influences in her/his exploration and adoption of technology. To be clear, this is not to suggest that instructors must demonstrate information literacy with all technology, but rather a willingness to understand, explore, and, when appropriate, implement too. According to Okojie (2011), it is important for teachers to be lifelong learners so that s/he can meet the needs and interests of students influenced by technology. Extending this argumentation, Nicholls (2000) asserts that instructors who are exposed to professional development that engages with the philosophy of lifelong learning are more likely to be intrinsically motivated to expand their knowledge to include technology in the classroom. Accordingly, such instructors are also more likely to instill a similar perspective of life learning in their students too. While the goal for a teacher to effectively deliver content in order for students to transfer and apply knowledge remains consistent, how technologies in the classroom foster life learning is worthy of future exploration. Especially given the technology-rich era and communities that we are immersed in.

More often than not, teachers are made aware of the possibilities of technology additives, supplements, and tools through professional development opportunities. Textbook publishers often offer virtual or in-person tutorials for media supplements (e.g., quizzes, activities, or assignments). For example, teachers maybe taught how to integrate e-Textbook supplements through their LMS or how to connect clickers for quizzes. However, rarely are teachers introduced to issues of *why* or for *what purpose or goal* such technological supplements serve their teaching or student learning (Price & Kirkwood, 2008). This reveals a potential problem with technology in the classroom in that it may be connected with teachers' uncertainties of its appropriateness both pedagogically and for student learning. That is, if a teacher is uncertain about *why* a technological tool enhances student learning, s/he is likely both less willing and ready to move forward with implementation in the classroom. Kirkwood and Price (2013) argue that teacher training programs must commit to understanding an instructor's pedagogical beliefs in order for technology to be effectively implemented for classroom use.

Concluding Thoughts

Many facets within the classroom have remained consistent through time; however, there are both foreseen and unforeseen changes on the horizon for education. From how students will access course content to how instructors will elicit feedback or meet students learning needs are all laden with possibilities for change. In short, as technology continues to rapidly change, so too will the landscape of the classroom in higher education. While students will more than likely see technology as well-suited for their learning, instructors will be tasked with assessing the pedagogical challenges of determining its appropriateness for the course. For instructors and higher education stakeholders like administrators (for further discussion, see Chapter 9), it may be worthwhile to consider how an instructor serves as a unifying bond within the classroom landscape. Finally, it is important to remember that even the most innovative instructor maybe constrained by other contextual factors such as department and university initiatives.

References

Boruszko, G. (2013). New technologies and teaching comparative literature. *Comparative Literature & Culture, 15*(6), 1–9.

Hedges, K. (2014, November 14). Six ways to avoid death by PowerPoint. Retrieved November 15, 2018, from https://www.forbes.com/sites/work-in-progress/2014/11/14/six-ways-to-avoid-death-by-powerpoint/

Hortsch, M. (2015). 'How we learn may not always be good for us'—Do new electronic teaching approaches always result in better learning outcomes? *Medical Teacher, 37*(6), 507–509. doi:10.3109/0142159X.2014.1001341

Hosek, A. M., & Titsworth, B. S. (2016). Scripting knowledge and experiences for millennial students. *Communication Education, 65*, 357–359. doi:10.1080/03634523.2016.1177844

Kirkwood, A., & Price, L. (2013). Missing: Evidence of a scholarly approach to teaching and learning with technology in higher education. *Teaching in Higher Education, 18*(3), 327–337. doi:10.1080/13562517.2013.773419

McCroskey, L. L., Richmond, V. P., & McCroskey, J. C. (2002). The scholarship of teaching and learning: Contributions from the discipline of communication. *Communication Education, 51*(4), 383.

Meloncon, L. (2007). Exploring electronic landscapes: Technical communication, online learning, and instructor preparedness. *Technical Communication Quarterly, 16*(1), 31–53. doi:10.1207/s15427625tcq1601_3

Mottet, T., & Beebe, S. A. (2006). Foundations of instructional communication. In T. Mottet, V. Richmond, & J. C. McCroskey (Eds.), *Handbook of instructional communication: Rhetorical and relational perspectives* (pp. 3–27). Boston, MA: Pearson.

76 Technology and Academic Audiences

Mottet, T., Richmond, V., & McCroskey, J. C. (2006). *Handbook of instructional Communication: Rhetorical and relational perspectives*. Boston, MA: Pearson.

Nicholls, G. (2000). Professional development, teaching, and lifelong learning: The implications for higher education. *International Journal of Lifelong Education, 19*(4), 370–377. doi:10.1080/02601370050110419

Okojie, M. C. (2011). The changing roles of teachers in a technology learning setting. *International Journal of Instructional Media, 38*(1), 17–25.

Price, L., & Kirkwood, A. (2008). Technology in the United Kingdom's higher education context. In S. Scott & K. C. Dixon (Eds.), *The globalised university: Trends and challenges in teaching and learning* (pp. 83–113). Perth: Black Swan Press. Retrieved from http://oro.open.ac.uk/11353/

Sellnow, D. D., Child, J. T., & Ahlfeldt, S. L. (2005). Textbook technology supplements: What are they good for? *Communication Education, 54*(3), 243–253. doi:10.1080/03634520500356360

9 Considerations for Administrators

Introduction

Institutions of higher education face uncertain futures with a variety of factors playing against them. Continued funding cuts from states, declining student enrollment, and questions of cost and quality of the education provided are all issues facing faculty and staff. For many administrators, the advent of affordable mobile devices and technology-based tools present a potential cost-savings to students and may serve as potential solutions to some of the issues facing higher education. However, this chapter cautions against moving too quickly into adopting technological solutions to problems facing higher education. For example, implementing a new technology program (i.e., iPads in the curriculum) can bring needed visibility and a sense of cutting-edge pedagogy to the institution; however, technology is not a perfect solution for all problems and these new technology programs can easily go awry. This chapter explores the benefits and challenges of decisions regarding technology on university campuses. This chapter will help administrators to understand different perspectives on technology initiatives they may be envisioning.

Mixed Views on Technology

As discussed in Chapter 7, faculty and administrators, particularly digital learning leaders, tend to have differing views on how effectively online classes compare to FtF ones. Jaschik and Lederman (2017) note that 55% of digital learning leaders agree that online courses can achieve equivalent learning outcomes as traditional courses, while only 11% of faculty agree. Parker, Lenhart and Moore (2011) report that over half of college presidents report that the educational value of online classes was roughly equal to traditional FtF classes. Taken together, these findings seem to indicate a rather large disparity

78 *Technology and Academic Audiences*

in views between faculty and administrators. One explanation could be how one's role at the university may affect perceptions of online classes. We caution administrators that their view of a technology or a technology as it is integrated into a curriculum may not be as strongly shared with faculty. This does not mean that one side is wrong and the other is right, but we would encourage both faculty and staff to discuss the reasoning behind their given perspective. Faculty may feel that online initiatives are being forced on them from upper adminstration, while administrators may feel that they are acting in the best interests of the institution and seeking to reduce the cost of attendance for students while also seeking to increase enrollment. Regardless of position at the institution, faculty and administrators both share in helping that institution to accomplish its educational mission.

Cautionary Tails

Administrators for a variety of educational institutions, as well as levels, likely have considered some sort of initiative to bring devices to students. For example, several high-profile cases have developed iPad initiatives for integrating those devices into the curriculum. These initiatives can be attractive for a variety of reasons, including positive publicity for the institution or school district, giving students hands-on experience with the latest technology and potentially streamlining the curriculum or freeing up instructors to provide more one-on-one time with students. However, several of these initiatives may not have lived up to expectations or provided evidence that a different approach may work better. Indeed, some initiatives even served as exemplars of how we might cautiously approach technology in the classroom. For example, Murphy (2014) writes about a New Jersey school district that, during 2012–2013, provided 200 students with iPads and 200 students with Chromebooks. After using the respective devices, the district sought student and teacher feedback and ultimately decided that the Chromebooks were a better fit for their need. The cautious approach discussed by Murphy (2014) is a good example of how to carefully consider technology in the classroom. However, technology does change at a quick rate, and many of the shortcoming identified by the school district (difficult to manage multiple iPads and lack of cloud support) appear to be have been added to the iPad or iOS operating system. Indeed, one of the main advantages of the Chromebook, identified in Murphy's article, was the integrated keyboard, which is something that Apple eventually added. For example, the current generation iPad Pro can be outfitted with a Smart Keyboard Folio that functions the same as the built-in keyboard of the Chromebook.

Considerations for Administrators 79

In a different example, in 2012, the University of Texas System developed an Institute for Transformational Learning that

> was envisioned as a kind of startup technology company that would create digital learning tools like a platform for health education, online courses available to people around the world and an iPad app that would let students access course materials.
> (Satija & Najmabadi, 2018, ¶. 2)

However, in 2018, after spending $75 million, the institute was closed. It appears as though the institute wasn't able to develop a model that secured long-term viability and, coupled with increased spending, the institute did not appear to be financially viable. Warner (2018), also writing about the University of Texas Institute of Transformational Learning, discusses other cases of innovations that did not live up to expectations. One of the cautions Warner (2018) provides is that:

> the purchaser of the product and the user of the product are two different groups. Schools and school systems buy the software, almost always relaying on the hype/marketing pitch of the providers. This allows lots of edtech products to get a foot in the door, but when they rubber hits the road in schools and the shortcomings become manifest, disillusion sets in quickly. Too many commercial edtech products are designed to past muster with administrations and boards to make that sale, rather than being rooted in real student needs.
> (¶. 29)

The disconnect between end user and purchaser is an important consideration to make. We argue that a critical component toward successfully implementing technology initiatives is a clear line of communication between teachers, students, and administrators prior to a final decision being made. In addition, each party needs to see a clear use for that initiative, one that is centered around student learning.

Practical Suggestions

One suggestion for administrators is to seek out faculty who are willing to pilot technology programs or initiatives in their classrooms. In addition, and just as important, is to provide incentive to faculty for the time and energy needed to develop new lesson plans, adjust curriculum, and work with students as they adjust to using a new device. As Warner (2018) noted, those responsible for purchasing technology

80 *Technology and Academic Audiences*

must be in clear contact with the end user. Whichever device or service is selected, it must have faculty buy in, and it must fulfill some sort of faculty or student need. Writing about avoiding failed higher education technology projects, Kubilus (2016) states

> All too often, the technology department of a college or university initiates a technology project—and obtains funding for it—without involving administration, faculty, staff, students, and others who will potentially be affected by the outcomes of the technology project.
>
> (¶. 4)

Similar to Warner's (2018), seeking buy in from stakeholders is a critical step that must not be overlooked.

Another suggestion focuses on the need that technology fulfills and how effectively that technology completes that need. We would caution administrators against quickly adopting a particular technology or software platform simply because it appears novel or attractive. While those can be attractive options, if they do not function well and are more complicated to use than the status quo, faculty and students may end up being frustrated or even refuse to use the new innovation.

Lastly, administrators should seek out faculty who are, on their own, starting to use different devices in the classroom and see how they can help those thought leaders. One potential result could be taking something that works in one or two classrooms and expanding that to other ones. This has the benefit of potentially demonstrating successful implementation in the classroom (i.e., it has already been pilot tested), and the faculty member responsible may support a wider implementation of their work.

Related to this suggestion is looking at what other institutions are doing. For example, faculty at Clemson University's Social Media Listening Center are using social media analysis software to analyze the social media activities of Russian agencies to see how those accounts may influence elections (Staton, 2019). Other universities are also developing centers and classes that examine social media content. For instance, Illinois State University created their Social Media Analytics Command Center (SMACC) in 2014. According to Denham (2014):

> Five School of Communication courses plan to use SMACC this semester, along with independent student and faculty researchers. One of the classes is Carpenter's Social Dynamics of Communication Technologies, which looks at how new technology impacts social institutions and social change.
>
> (¶. 6)

Such centers serve as examples of how a new technology or innovation can be successfully integrated into the curriculum. Often times, these centers not only facilitate classroom learning but also allow faculty and students to engage in cutting-edge research that would not otherwise be possible.

One important point to make is the diverging views from administrators at the postsecondary and K-12 levels. Given the different expectations and nature of these different educational levels, we would expect administrators to, understandably, have different points of views or areas of emphasis. For example, college or university administrators might place more emphasis on faculty having access to technology resources for conducting research. Meanwhile, K-12 administrators might be more attuned to teachers and students having devices in class to facilitate learning. While we use examples, in this chapter and in others, from both educational levels, our perspective and suggestions are routed in our experiences as faculty. Thus, this chapter is best viewed in that light, suggestions to administrators from faculty.

Conclusion

Higher education is one area that will likely continue to benefit from new innovations; however, the adoption of technology into the classroom must be done cautiously. At times, it appears as though new technologies or systems have been introduced without gaining the support of faculty or students, and this can often lead to less than desirable results. Instead, we suggest that administrators carefully consider which technology to invest in but, even more importantly, work with faculty and students to make sure that any technology brought into the institution is supported and wanted by stakeholders. Worth also considering is the rapid pace with which technology evolves and changes. As noted earlier in this chapter, a New Jersey school district opted to use Chromebooks instead of iPads, because the Chromebooks better fit their needs (Murphy, 2014). However, both Chromebooks and iPads have changed over the years, and perhaps the school districts needs have changed as well. Thus, administrators not only need to cautiously approach technology, but they also need to be willing to revisit those decisions and reevaluate their needs.

References

Denham, R. (2014, September 13). *Illinois state launches social media analytics command center.* Retrieved from https://news.illinoisstate.edu/2014/09/illinois-state-launches-social-media-analytics-command-center/

82 Technology and Academic Audiences

Jaschik, S., & Lederman, D. (2017). *2017 survey of faculty attitudes on technology: A study by Inside Higher Ed and Gallup.* Retrieved from https://www.insidehighered.com/booklet/2017-survey-faculty-attitudes-technology

Kubilus, N. J. (2016, June 27). *Avoiding failure with higher education technology projects.* Retrieved from https://er.educause.edu/articles/2016/6/avoiding-failure-with-higher-education-technology-projects

Murphy, M. (2014, August 4). *Why some schools are selling all their iPads: Four years after Apple introduced its popular tablet, many districts are switching to laptops.* Retrieved from https://www.theatlantic.com/education/archive/2014/08/whats-the-best-device-for-interactive-learning/375567/

Parker, K., Lenhart, A., & Moore, K. (2011). *The digital revolution and higher education: College presidents, public differ on value of online learning.* Retrieved from http://www.pewresearch.org/wp-content/uploads/sites/3/2011/08/online-learning.pdf

Satija, N., & Najmabadi, S. (2018, February 7). *"Costly and unsustainable:" After spending $75 million, a troubled UT System technology institute shuts its doors.* Retrieved from https://www.texastribune.org/2018/02/07/ut-system-shuts-down-major-endowment-funded-initiative/

Staton, M. (2019, January 11). *Researchers study activity of Russian 'trolls'.* Retrieved from https://clemson.world/researchers-study-activity-of-russian-trolls/

Warner, J. (2018, February 15). *The high cost of failed innovation.* Retrieved from https://www.insidehighered.com/blogs/just-visiting/high-cost-failed-innovation

10 Considerations for Students

Introduction

We know that past studies provide evidence for technology both helping and hurting student learning (see Part 2 of this book). The general finding appears to be that when used for non-class-related purposes, technology hurts learning. When used for things related to the class or class content, technology may be able to help in the learning process and provide students with valuable skills and experiences with using technology. Practically speaking, students' use of technology in class can certainly be helpful. For example, electronic notes can help students to efficiently take notes from class that they can easily refer back to later on; however, students need to resist the tendency to simply take verbatim notes (Mueller & Oppenheimer, 2014). In addition, we know that having notebook computers in class may be distracting for the student and students seated around that individual (Sana, Weston, & Cepeda, 2013). We also know that students can and do use their notebook computers for multitasking and those multitasking behaviors are often distracting in nature (Kraushaar & Novak, 2010). Despite the potential for negative effects on learning, technology can still be used to help enhance learning. As instructors, with decades of teaching experience between the three of us, and communication scholars, we offer the following as considerations for students regarding how they may use, or not use, technology in their classes.

Student Behaviors

Perhaps our primary suggestion is entirely within a student's hands and that is self-regulating one's use of technology in the classroom. This isn't necessarily a new concept, many of the behaviors we see regarding student use of technology in the classroom appear to be the modern equivalents of existing behaviors. For example, students

84   *Technology and Academic Audiences*

staring out the window is not that different from students scrolling through their Twitter feed. Just as in the past, students can combat this by being disciplined and preventing their own behaviors that lead to distractive activities. This includes how and when they use their mobile devices, particularly when they are in the classroom. We aren't suggesting students completely abstain from device usage during the day, merely that they regulate their usage while in class. Wei, Wang, and Klausner (2012) found that student self-regulation could help to sustain attention in the classroom and lead to cognitive learning. From our own research (Kuznekoff, Munz, & Titsworth, 2015; Kuznekoff & Titsworth, 2013), we know that students who abstained from using their devices or used their devices for course-relevant messaging did not suffer the same decreases in learning as those actively using their mobile devices. Ultimately, it is up to students to engage in appropriate device use, just as students are expected to focus on the course content and instructor.

Another suggestion for students is to keep their device usage focused on the class. If using a mobile device or notebook computer in the classroom, students should keep the use of that device centered on classroom learning and not for multitasking (Kraushaar & Novak, 2010). We know that it can often be tempting for students to briefly look at their messaging app or to check a social networking site or two; however, that can easily lead to the student focusing on content outside the classroom and unrelated to the topic at hand (i.e., serve as a distraction). Thus, students should carefully consider how and when they use their devices in class. We would also recommend asking faculty how they view technology in class. Many faculty likely support appropriate student use of mobile devices in class; however, other faculty may ask students to not bring or use their devices in class. We do encourage both faculty and students to discuss how technology can and should be used in the classroom and situations in which this usage should vary.

Transferring Skills to the Workplace

College is one of the last environments in which students can experiment with and practice behaviors and skills that they will use in the workplace, and this includes technology. This sentiment does not focus simply on proficiency with particular programs or applications. Instead, this idea includes the general behaviors surrounding technology use, particularly in a professional context. Some organizations might encourage texting between coworkers or use a messaging app

Considerations for Students 85

like Slack for internal communication and many workplaces likely encourage employees to use their mobile devices to keep in close contact with coworkers. However, other workplaces may take a different approach and value the face-to-face interactions that occur in team or department meetings. Simons (2018), in an article in *The Wall Street Journal*, discusses employers who banned mobile phones during meetings, noting that this appears to be a complex issue without a singular solution. However, some employers were growing discouraged with employees attending meetings and spending that time on their mobile devices. While accessing information to inform discussion is an appropriate use of technology in a meeting, it would seem that many people are also using that technology to access content that is unrelated to the meeting agenda.

This behavior also appears to echo experiences that faculty have in the classroom, specifically when students use mobile devices to access content unrelated to class content. As noted by Simons (2018), some managers are outright banning mobile devices in meetings, and we also see evidence of this happening in higher education settings as well. For example, Berdik (2018) reports that "since fall 2016, the communications department at California State University at Dominguez Hills has banned smartphones, laptops and other personal technology in every classroom—with grade deductions for violations—except for teacher-guided use and 'tech breaks' during longer classes" (¶. 3). While outright ban of mobile devices in the classroom and during meetings is likely rare, it does appear to be a potential trend. Worth considering is how individuals use their own devices while at work, and this can be a period of self-reflection for individuals. If one is using their devices productively to access information and as a tool to accomplish work related tasks, then we should continue to allow devices in the classroom and during meetings. However, it is up to individuals to self-monitor their device usage, and if they are using their mobile devices to "zone out" during meetings, we would suggest they carefully consider the ramifications of that action.

Conclusion

At present, we would argue that the classroom and workplace are still grappling with how to adapt to an increasing mediated educational and work environment. Each classroom and organization is different, possessing its own unique culture and that also applies to how the use of technology fits into that culture. Certainly, some of this adaptation includes older generations adapting to a new generation, but the

86 *Technology and Academic Audiences*

inverse of this is also true. In particular to higher education, the college classroom was forced to evolve over the past 20–30 years and technology has likely been one of the driving forces in this evolution. These changes are generally positive, but we would caution students to remember that this is still an unfolding process. Each classroom and workplace is different, and we would encourage students to adapt to each of these environments accordingly, particularly when it comes to how to use or not use technology. Ultimately, it will fall on the student to carefully reflect on and self-monitor their own technology use.

References

Berdik, C. (2018, January 22). *To ban or not to ban: Teachers grapple with forcing students to disconnect from technology.* Retrieved from https://www.washingtonpost.com/news/grade-point/wp/2018/01/22/to-ban-or-not-to-ban-teachers-cope-with-students-driven-to-distraction-by-technology/?utm_term=.974935a13230

Kraushaar, J. M., & Novak, D. C. (2010). Examining the affects of student multitasking with laptops during the lecture. *Journal of Information Systems Education, 21,* 241–251.

Kuznekoff, J. H., Munz, S. M., & Titsworth, B. S. (2015). Mobile phones in the classroom: Examining the effects of texting, Twitter, and message content on student learning. *Communication Education, 64,* 344–365. doi:10.1080/03634523.2015.1038727

Kuznekoff, J. H., & Titsworth, B. S. (2013). The impact of mobile phone usage on student learning. *Communication Education, 62,* 233–252. doi:10.1080/03634523.2013.767917

Mueller, P. A., & Oppenheimer, D. M. (2014). The pen is mightier than the keyboard: Advantages of longhand over laptop note taking. *Psychological Science, 25,* 1159–1168. doi:10.1177/0956797614524581

Sana, F., Weston, T., & Cepeda, N. J. (2013). Laptop multitasking hinders classroom learning for both users and nearby peers. *Computers & Education, 62,* 24–31. doi:10.1016/j.compedu. 2012.10.003

Simons, J. (2018, May 16). 'I lost it': *The boss who banned phones, and what came next.* Retrieved from https://www.wsj.com/articles/can-you-handle-it-bosses-ban-cellphones-from-meetings-1526470250

Wei, F. F., Wang, Y. K., & Klausner, M. (2012). Rethinking college students' self-regulation and sustained attention: Does text messaging during class influence cognitive learning? *Communication Education, 61,* 185–204.

11 Conclusion

How we use technology to enable learning is a hotly debated question and thriving area of research across a variety of disciplines. We fully expect that this area of research will continue to expand and adapt to a changing technological landscape. This continuing area of research will enable teachers, administrators, and students to make informed, evidence-based decisions about how we can use technology to enhance learning; and when it may be advisable to restrict the use of technology in the classroom. Without question, ignoring the impact of technology on higher education is an unsustainable approach and more research across a variety of learning contexts is certainly needed. For example, we have encountered faculty who opt to ban technology from their classrooms and others who embrace a more laissez faire system that allows students to use as much or little technology as s/he wishes. While instructors may view this approach as appropriate, we would argue that outright bans on technology likely do not represent a modern lifestyle or working environment. Instead, we firmly believe that technology has an important place in P-12 and university education levels. This does not mean that technology must be integrated into our curriculum at all times or at every grade level. We would argue that educators should carefully integrate technology into the classroom in meaningful ways, paying careful attention to student learning as well as existing access or barriers. Beginning with carefully considering what technology could be used in the classroom and also understanding how that usage will be done in a thoughtful way, educators can focus on meaningful integration.

One potential way of taking a step toward meaningful technological integration in the classroom is through careful selection of which technologies may best enable student learning. Often times, we have witnessed instructors quickly integrate a new mobile device application (or app) into the classroom; however, this runs the risk of

88 *Technology and Academic Audiences*

appearing as a gimmick or simply using the latest app, without carefully thinking through how that app may function in the classroom or facilitate learning. Some apps and technology can appear as an attractive option, but without carefully considering how the technology will be used to help students learn, those initiatives will likely fail. In order for this approach to succeed, faculty need to give students instruction in what to do with technology and how to do it but also with space for students to develop their own way of reaching learning outcomes. For example, an elementary school class may have the assignment of developing a book report on different species of trees in the local community. Using tablets and collaborative software, students could take photos of trees in their community and videos of wildlife found around those trees and integrate this content into their own e-Book or interactive presentation. In another example, students might be asked to work with a local community group to increase their social media presence. Those students might use mobile phones to record and edit short videos or use editing software to develop still images for a social media campaign. Taken together, both of these examples illustrate how technology can be used as an educational tool that enables learning and not the focal point of the assignment or lesson.

Teachers at a variety of educational levels are using technology to help enhance learning and deeply engage students in the learning process. However, we do caution against viewing technology as a "cure all" for teacher-challenges (e.g., evaluation, procedural, practicality, and power challenges, see Simonds, Wright, & Cooper, 2019). For example, prior chapters of this book have discussed how some iPad or laptop initiatives either failed or were unsuccessful in meeting expected learning outcomes. We would argue that this is likely because technology was simply applied to the problem and not tightly integrated with learning or classroom instruction. In other words, providing universal access to technology for all students (through tablets or notebook computers) is insufficient in enabling learning. Not only must access be guaranteed, but students must also be provided with instruction on how to use these devices.

Equally important and worthy of consideration is training and education for teachers and faculty. In order to meaningfully integrate technology into a curriculum, teachers must have a thorough understanding and, potentially, an expertise in the technology used in the classroom. For example, Apple developed the Apple Teacher program (https://www.apple.com/education/apple-teacher/) that provides teachers with not only professional development training with different products and apps but also guidance for how the products

Conclusion 89

and apps can be used in the classroom. This approach provides teachers with the knowledge and expertise in using that technology, as well as assistance in meaningfully integrating the technology into the curriculum. Microsoft has a similar program called Microsoft Education (https://www.microsoft.com/en-us/education/educators/default.aspx), which includes content focused for educators and, we suspect, that other major tech companies have similar programs. We would encourage teachers and faculty to seek out these programs to not only enhance their own knowledge about technology in the classroom but primarily to help inform how they plan to use technology in the classroom.

Another point of caution we offer is to avoid quickly integrating a new app or feature into the curriculum, without carefully considering the role that technology plays in the learning process. Often times, it is relatively easy to get swept up in the latest and greatest trend in educational technology; however, we would suggest that instructors carefully reflect on how they use technology and view this as an evolutionary process. For example, we know instructors who have implemented shared note-taking in class and used free, cross platform apps to facilitate that note-taking. In this circumstance, students in class would collectively take digital notes that each student could contribute to or edit. In some cases, such an approach is successful and likely aided student learning; however, in other circumstances the online note-taking morphed into a separate conversation which may have distracted from the class discussion that day. The creation of two distinct, simultaneously occurring conversations, could have the effect of negatively influencing learning, although additional research is needed to examine this issue more fully. Although we applaud teachers who experiment with integrating technology in the classroom, this point of caution is still worthy of consideration.

While the content in this chapter highlights points of caution, we do remain cautiously optimistic and encourage faculty who wish to experiment with technology in their classrooms. We would argue that it is only through pilot testing and thoughtful reflection that educators will continue to develop best practices for technology in the classroom. We also note that many of these initiatives will fail or, at the very least, not produce the expected outcomes. Educators need to be not only prepared for such an outcome but also willing to carefully consider what worked or did not work. It is also worthy of considering how our students feel about technology. That is, what are their preferences? And further, how can we balance a forward-thinking approach to learning with technology, while remaining mindful of

90 *Technology and Academic Audiences*

well-researched and effective instructional practices. Failure is a learning experience that can help us identify what could be done differently and how we might improve for next time. Only then, can we explore or consider further possibilities to enhance a student's learning experience in the classroom.

At this point, we simply can't ignore technology in the classroom. Mobile devices and computers have become a fundamental aspect of everyday life. We would argue that educators can not only use technology to help aid learning but also model how students should use technology in their lives outside of school. In particular, college is where students can learn how to use tech effectively in a work environment and to do so in a fairly supportive environment. As educators, we can help students to do this and help guide them as technology evolves and changes.

Reference

Simonds, C. J., Wright, A. M., & Cooper, P. J. (2019). *Communication for teachers & trainers*. Southlake, TX: Fountainhead Press.

Index

Ackerman, R. 53, 54
active learning classrooms (ALCs) 41–3
administrators: educational administrators 19; face-to-face (FtF) courses 60; and faculty 78; K-12 levels 81; postsecondary 81; practical suggestions 79–81; technology 77–8, 80
Ahlfeldt, S. L. 72
ALCs *see* active learning classrooms
Alexander, P. A. 55
Allen, I. E. 59
Apple 4, 78, 88
Apple's Keynote slideshow 70
augmented and virtual reality (AR/VR) technology 43–6

Bailey, J. H. 41
Bandwith Recovery (Verschelden) 37, 45
Baron, N. S. 55
Bayliss, L. 53
Berdik, C. 85
Blackboard discussions 61
Boruszko, G. 71
boyd, d. 21
Bring Your Own Device (BYOD) principles 38
Brown, C. 18, 20
Bryne, A. 29

Calarco, J. M. 62
Campbell, S. W. 11
cell phone use 37; *see also* mobile phones; smartphones

Cepeda, N. J. 13
Chandrasekera, T. 43
Child, J. T. 72
Chromebooks 78
classrooms: active learning 41–3; communication messages 71; computers in 9; devices in 10, 80; educational benefits in 69; email and/or LMS announcements 62; e-readers 52; gender stereotyping 31; innovative 41; instructor pedagogy 69, 71; iPads for 4; K-12 45; laptops/notebooks in 13–15; latest app or device in 4; learning 84; learning tools in 45; lecture-style 41; mobile phones in 5, 9, 11–13, 38; online 58, 59–63; physically present in 59; speaks to female students 32; student self-regulation 83, 84; tablets 52; teachers and students relationships 71; teaching practices in 69, 70; technology-free 72; technology in 3, 9, 10, 15–16, 70–1, 74; texting behaviors in 11; traditional FtF 62; twenty-first century 5; utilize technology 73
CMC *see* computer-mediated communication
Cocker, J. 61
Cohen, D. 27
college classroom 4, 11, 86
communication: computer-mediated communication (CMC) 26; discipline 9, 11; instructional communication 10;

92 Index

parent-teacher communication 26; between teachers, students, and administrators 79
computer-mediated communication (CMC) 26
Connell, C. 53, 54
Cotton, S. R. 31
Czerniewicz, L. 18, 20

Dailey, D. 29
Daniel, D. B. 52
Davies, J. 61
De Bruyckere, P. 19
Denham, R. 80
digital bind 31
digital differentiation 25, 26
digital divide 25–7; university classroom 24
digital immigrants 19, 49
digital inequality 27–8; ethnicity 31; income level 31; individual predicators of 30; race 31; university classroom 28
digital learning leaders 60, 77
digital literacy 27–8
digital literacy skills 24–5
digital native: assumptions 4, 21–2; define 18–19; and digital immigrant students 49; and digital literacy 21; problematization 19–21; skill gaps 4

e-Book 49–51, 53, 55, 88
E-Sports 42, 43
e-Textbooks 32, 49–53, 55, 70, 74; vs. print reading 53–5
ethnicity 27, 30–1
evidence-based research 69, 87

Facebook 11, 20
Facebook's Oculus Rift 43
face-to-face (FtF) courses 28, 60, 70
Farmer, W. 53
Federal Communications Commission (FCC) 38
flipped classroom 29, 41, 42
Flores, J. 51

Gardiner, S. 46
gender identity 27, 28, 31–2, 37, 45

global educational technology market 4
Goldsmith, M. 53, 54
Gonzales, A. L. 25, 29, 62
Google Cardboard 44, 45
Google glasses 44
Gordy, X. Z. 41
Grady, E. F. 26
Graff, M. 61

hardcopy book 49–51, 54
Harter, L. 38–40
Hartman, J. A. 16
hashtag 42
Hogan, P. 15
Hong, K. 21
Hortsch, M. 70
Hosek, A. M. 71

Immersive Media Initiative (IMI) 44
Inman, C. 16
innovation: digital 56; tradition and 50
innovative classroom 41
Institute for Transformational Learning 79
Internet 20; for social support activities 31; younger users 22
iPads 4, 10, 54, 78
iPhone 24

Jaschik, S. 59, 77
Jelenewicz, S. M. 31
Johnson, G. M. 56
Jones, C. 19
Jones, E. M. 41

K-12 administrators 81
K-12 classrooms 45
Kindle (Amazon's e-reader) 50, 54
Kirkwood, A. 72, 74
Kirschner, P. A. 19
Klausner, M. 11, 84
Kraushaar, J. M. 11, 14
Kubilus, N. J. 80

Lai, K. 21
L.A. Unified School District 4, 10
learning focused technology and pedagogy approach 72

Index 93

learning management systems (LMSs) 61, 62, 71, 74
Lederman, D. 59, 77
Lenhart, A. 77
life course approach 28
Littlejohn, A. 20
Lubke, J. K. 51, 52
Lynch, T. 62

Margaryan, A. 20
massive open online courses (MOOCs) 70
Mazer, J. P. 26
Meloncon, L. 72
Merkoski, J. 50
messaging app 84
Microsoft 89
Microsoft's PowerPoint 70
mobile phones 5, 9, 11–13, 38; negatively impact student attention 9
modern classroom 3–4
MOOCs see massive open online courses
Moore, K. 77
Mueller, P. A. 14, 15
Murphy, M. 78

National Center for Education Statistics 58
Newton, D. 60
Nicholas, A. 22
Nicholls, G. 74
Nicol, A. A. M. 42
note-taking 9, 11, 14, 42, 55, 89
Novak, D. C. 11, 14

O'Bannon, B. W. 51, 52
Occulus Go headsets 43
Oculus Rift 3
Ohio State University (OSU) 4
Ohio University (OU) 10
Okojie, M. C. 74
online assignments 28
online classroom 58–63
online content creation 30
online course registration 9
online degree programs 59, 63
online education 59, 63, 64

online learning 15; classroom 60–2; deconstructing 59–60; growth of 58–9; higher education 60; leaders 60; negative aspects of 59; programs 63
online multimedia storytelling project 42
online teaching 58
online, womens in social support activities 31–2
Oppenheimer, D. M. 14, 15

parent-teacher communication 26
Parker, K. 63, 77
P-12 classroom education 26
Pearson 10
Photoshop editing 39
Pokemon Go 44
Powell, A. 29
Prensky, M. 18–21
Price, L. 72, 74
problem-solving skills 40

race 27, 28, 30–1, 37, 45
recall 9, 11; of information 5, 13, 54
Robinson, L. 26–8, 30
Rockinson-Szapkiw, A. J. 54

Sana, F. 13–14
Schulz, J. 28
Seaman, J. 59
Sellnow, D. D. 72
Simoni, Z. R. 30
Simons, J. 85
Singer, L. M. 55
Skolits, G. J. 51, 52
small open online courses (SMOOCs) 70
Smart Keyboard Folio 78
smartphones 24, 26, 29, 39, 44–6, 85
Smith, A. 22
SMOOCs see small open online courses
social inequalities 25
Social media 10, 22, 40, 46, 52, 73, 80, 88
Social Media Analytics Command Center (SMACC) 80
social networking sites (SNSs) 31

94 *Index*

socioeconomic status (SES) 21, 24, 26, 28–9, 62
software: administrators 80; for non-course-related purposes 11; Pearson 10; social media 80, 88; use of students 15, 16
Stallard, C. K. 61
students: academic experiences 26; ALC classroom 46; AR/VR content 46; attention 9; behaviors 14, 83–4; digital immigrant 49; digital native 18–20, 49; e-Book 49; enhance learning 3, 5; e-Textbooks 49; face-to-face (FtF) courses 60; female student 32; iPads 78; learning 5, 9, 50, 51–3, 69–71, 75; multitasking 14, 52; note-taking behaviors 9, 11, 14; one-on-one time 78; P-12 students 26; race and ethnicity 31; recall 9, 11, 13; self-regulation 83, 84; socioeconomic factors 28, 29; technology 73; transferring skills to workplace 84–5; #turnitgold 38–40, 46; using devices in classroom 10
Sun, J. 51

Tanguma, J. 51
teachers: ALC classes 41, 42; AR/VR technology 45, 46; cell phone use, policy restrictions of 37; computer-mediated communication (CMC) 26; digital native 19; education software system 10; K-12 classrooms 45; pedagogy 72–3; preparation and technology 73–4; technology in classroom 70–1; training programs 74

teaching-focused technology and pedagogy approach 72
technology and learning: online classroom 58; problem with 4–5
technology-free classroom 72
Thomas, M. 21
Thompson, B. C. 26
Titsworth, B. S. 71
traditional classrooms 3, 42, 62
traditional FtF classroom 62, 63, 77
#turnitgold 38–40, 46
Twitter 12, 42, 84

university classroom 24–6, 28, 49, 50, 52, 53, 55
University of Texas Institute of Transformational Learning 79

Venmo 40
Verschelden, C. 37, 38, 45, 46
virtual classroom 60
Virtual reality (VR) 3
visual communication 40, 42
Vojt, G. 20

The Wall Street Journal 85
Wang, Y. K. 11, 84
Warburton, S. 15
Warner, J. 79, 80
web-based learning 70
Wei, F. F. 11, 84
Weisberg, M. 50, 52
Weston, T. 13
Wiborg, O. 28
Wood, E. 14
Woody, W. D. 52
Wright, V. H. 16

Yoon, S. Y. 43
Young, J. R. 15